The Promise-Powered Life

How to See the Promises of God Fulfilled in Your Life

J. M. FARRO

Scripture quotations marked NIV are taken from THE HOLY BIBLE, NEW INTERNATIONAL VERSION®, NIV® Copyright © 1973, 1978, 1984, 2011 by Biblica, Inc.™ Used by permission. All rights reserved worldwide.

Scripture quotations marked AMP are taken from the Amplified Bible. Copyright © 1954, 1958, 1962, 1964, 1965, 1987 by The Lockman Foundation. Used by permission.

Scripture quotations marked NASB are taken from the NEW AMERICAN STANDARD BIBLE®. © Copyright 1960, 1962, 1963, 1968, 1971, 1972, 1973, 1975, 1977, 1995 by The Lockman Foundation. Used by permission.

Scripture quotations marked NKJV are taken from the New King James Version. Copyright © 1982 by Thomas Nelson, Inc. Used by permission. All rights reserved.

Scripture quotations marked THE MESSAGE are taken from THE MESSAGE. Copyright (c) by Eugene H. Peterson 1993, 1994, 1995, 1996, 2000, 2001, 2002. Used by permission of NavPress Publishing Group.

Scripture quotations marked NLT are taken from the Holy Bible, New Living Translation. Copyright 1996, 2004. Used by permission of Tyndale House Publishers, Inc., Wheaton, Illinois 60189. All rights reserved.

Verses marked TLB are taken from The Living Bible. Copyright 1971. Used by permission of Tyndale House Publishers, Inc., Wheaton, Illinois 60189. All rights reserved.

Copyright © 2013 by J. M. FARRO
P.O. Box 434
Nazareth, PA 18064

Printed in the United States of America. All rights reserved under International Copyright Law. Contents and /or cover may not be reproduced in whole or in part in any form without the written consent of the Author.

ISBN: 1484060393

ISBN-13: 978-1484060391

Acknowledgements

I would like to take this opportunity to thank my husband, Joe, for helping me to put this project together, and for faithfully reading and editing my devotionals on a regular basis. I could not devote myself to my ministry work without his constant support and understanding. He has been my best friend and confidant for more than 40 years.

I also sincerely appreciate my son, Joseph, and all of the valuable technical support and computer help he has given me over the years. His expertise, confidence, and calmness in stressful times have been a great inspiration and encouragement to me.

A special thanks to my son, John, who has allowed me to serve on the staff of his extraordinary ministry, Jesusfreakhideout.com, for the past 16 years. I am ever so grateful to him for telling me those many years ago, "Mom, you should write some devotionals for my site..."

Cover Photo by Joseph DiBiase II

Introduction

When I got serious about my relationship with Christ twenty years ago, and began an in-depth study of the Scriptures, I discovered that I had inherited a wealth of promises from God Himself. I also discovered that these divine promises are not automatic. They have to be claimed and received by faith.

As I sought the Lord about receiving the full benefit of His promises, He showed me His instructions in Isaiah 62:6-7 (AMP): "You who [are His servants and by your prayers] put the Lord in remembrance [of His promises], keep not silence, and give Him no rest..." One of the best ways to activate the power and benefits of God's supernatural promises is to pray them back to the Lord. When we do this, we are in effect telling Him, "Lord, this is what You said, and I'm trusting You to keep Your Word."

Since I began making my prayers promise-centered, instead of problem-centered, I have seen my percentage of answered prayer increase dramatically. Why? Because when we pray God's promises, we are praying God's will. And the Bible says that "if we ask anything according to His will, He hears us," and we can be confident "that we have what we asked of Him". (1 John 5:14-15 NIV)

The Lord has given His children promises of provision, protection, power, deliverance, life, healing, strength, wisdom, peace, joy, victory, success, wholeness, freedom, and everything we need to live the abundant life in Christ, and to fulfill our God-given purpose and potential on this earth.

Scripture says that Jesus "carries out and fulfills all of God's promises, no matter how many of them there are". (2 Corinthians 1:20 TLB) I encourage you to dig into God's Word, asking the Lord to lead you to the promises that pertain to your specific needs. Believe them. Pray them. Claim them as your own. Then watch God go to work to prove His faithfulness every time!

Table of Contents

A SIGNIFICANT LIFE 1

CHILDLIKE FAITH 5

TRUTH FOR YOUR LOVED ONES 9

COMFORT AND JOY 13

GOD'S VERY BEST 17

THE GOD OF INCREASE 21

GOD WILL WORK 25

GOD'S HEALING REPORT 27

EXCEEDINGLY ABUNDANTLY 29

THE REWARDS OF FORGIVENESS 33

OUR MIGHTY WARRIOR 37

NO REGRETS 39

GOD'S EMPOWERMENT 43

HOLD FAST 45

EXPLOITS FOR GOD 49

GOD CARES 53

BUILD ON THE ROCK 55

NEVER GIVE UP 57

DON'T FAIL TO ASK 59

FEARLESS	61
LATER AND GREATER	63
EVERY DISEASE	65
SPEEDY WORKS	67
GOOD MORNINGS	69
THE LION'S DEN	71
DIVINE PROTECTION	73
SAYING GOODBYE	75
BLESSING-FILLED SLEEP	77
FROM TEARS TO JOY	79
OUR HEAVENLY GUARD	83
WORLD CHANGERS FOR CHRIST	85
SEEING EYES	89
WISDOM FOR RELATIONSHIPS	93
MOUNTAIN MOVERS	97
OVERCOMING POWER	99
SUPERNATURAL REVELATION	103
STRONG IN GOD	107
RELIEF AND REDRESS	111
REWARDS FOR SERVICE	113
OUR HEART'S DESIRES	117

DECLARE AND ESTABLISH YOUR VICTORY	121
PERFECT PEACE	123
SUPERHUMAN ENERGY	127
CLOSED DOORS	131
PEACEFUL DWELLINGS	135
SOW HIS PROMISES	137
A QUICK RECOVERY	139
UNFAMILIAR PATHS	141
DOOM THE DEVOURER	143
SKILLS BLESSED BY GOD	145
FORGET THE CRISIS PRAYERS	147
FREEDOM AND HEALING	151
GOD'S GOT ANOTHER OPTION	155
COMPLAINTS, DOUBTS, AND HIGHEST PURPOSES	157
"DISCREET" DECISIONS	161
ABOUT THE AUTHOR	165

A Significant Life

"Humble yourselves [feeling very insignificant] in the presence of the Lord, and He will exalt you [He will lift you up and make your lives significant]." James 4:10 AMP

When I surrendered my life to the Lord in earnest twenty years ago, I had no trouble "feeling very insignificant". I had been a stay-at-home mom for many years, and I didn't have any marketable skills or training to speak of. What I did have, however, was a willing heart. I wanted so much to make a difference for God in this world, and I asked Him to put me to work in His Kingdom.

Before too long, he led my oldest son, Joseph, to launch a Bible club in his public high school. I volunteered to become the official "club mom," and I took on the responsibility of providing biblical teachings, refreshments, and transportation for the students involved. It was hard, and often thankless, work. But I loved the fact that I was laboring for the Lord, and drawing others – especially teens – to Him. When God made a way for me to be on national radio with a Congressman, I rejoiced that I was finally getting some real recognition and appreciation.

When both of my sons graduated from high school, and my family's involvement with the Bible club ceased, I felt lost. Again, I pleaded with the Lord to put me to work in His kingdom, and this time, He led me to join the staff of my son, John's, Christian music web site. At first, all I did was answer prayer requests. Then John asked me to write some devotionals for his site. To be honest, I became indignant when my son made the request, but when my emotions settled down, I sought the Lord for His will in the matter. When it became clear that God wanted me to honor John's request, I began writing devotionals, and mailing out a weekly newsletter for my subscribers. As the Lord graciously allowed me to reach more and more people with His life-changing truth through my newsletters, books, and podcasts, I rejoiced that I was once again making a difference for His Kingdom.

God knows that we have a desire to feel significant. But He wants our significance to come from Him. Maybe you are struggling with feeling insignificant today. Please know that wherever you are, whatever your age, whatever your circumstance, God has awesome plans for you. He longs to lift you up, and to give you a life of true purpose and meaning. Seek Him today. Make yourself available to Him. As you make His plans for you your own, you will see the fulfillment of His Word!

Lord, I believe that You have specific plans and purposes for my life, and I don't want to miss out on a single one. Direct my steps, and redirect them, if necessary, so that I will always walk in Your perfect will. I know that in the center of Your will is where I will enjoy a life of significance. Today, I choose to leave my own agenda behind, and to lay hold of the awesome plans You have for me!

Promise-Power Point:** **When I humble myself and follow God's agenda, He will make my life significant for His glory.

Childlike Faith

"Let the children come to Me. Don't stop them! For the Kingdom of God belongs to such as these. I assure you, anyone who doesn't have their kind of faith will never get into the Kingdom of God." Mark 10:14-15 NLT

When my children were growing up, our family raised guinea pigs as pets. My son, John, and I were usually the ones who gave them the most attention, and who most cared for them. When our last guinea pig, Daisy, died, I was so heartbroken that I announced to my family that we were not going to have any more pets. Everyone seemed fine with my decision except my son, John. He was devastated, and for months afterwards, he pleaded with me to let him have another pet. But I stood firm and refused time and time again.

What I didn't know during that time was that John was earnestly praying for a new pet. And the Lord went about providing him with one in His own creative and amazing way. Early one Spring, a mother duck made her nest and laid her eggs on our back porch. When she abandoned her nest after only a week or two, my husband, Joe, decided to bring the eggs inside to try to hatch them. When two adorable little ducklings popped out one day, my family and I were elated, and no one was happier than John. He doted on those ducks and nurtured them tenderly. And since that day thirteen years ago, my family and I have been raising pet ducks.

Sometimes when I am praying and trusting God in a situation where the odds are stacked against me, the Lord reminds me how He provided my son with pets when everything made that seem extremely unlikely. In the promise above in Mark 10, Jesus tells us that having the faith of a child is the kind of faith we need to get into His Kingdom. What the Lord has also taught me is that we often need the same kind of trusting faith to receive our daily provision and protection from Him.

If it's healing we need, having the faith of a child can enable us to believe God for a miracle, even when the diagnosis is grim. If it's financial or material needs that are on our minds, having this kind of simple, trusting faith can lead us to ask for abundance, when we can hardly even pay our bills. And if it's restoration for a relationship that is our heart's desire, it's the faith of a child that can inspire us to ask and believe God to do the impossible. If the Lord could send a mother duck to lay eggs on my back porch to fulfill a praying child's request for a pet, how much more could He do for you, if you'd ask Him in faith?

Lord, forgive me for the times I've been too proud, cynical, or skeptical to ask You for the things I need or desire. Give me a trusting heart, and teach me how to pray simple, believing prayers. Deliver me from worldly thinking, and renew my mind to Your truth. Thank You that as I demonstrate the faith of a child, I will see You move mountains on my behalf!

Promise-Power Point: *If I will pray and trust God with childlike faith, I will witness the Lord's power and provision on my behalf.*

Truth for Your Loved Ones

"Those who err in mind will know the truth, and those who criticize will accept instruction." Isaiah 29:24 NASB

This is one of the promises I prayed and stood on for my family when I first dedicated my life to the Lord. At the time, my husband, Joe, and I had been married for almost twenty years, and our sons were 15 and 12 years old. Needless to say, my family and I had not been walking with the Lord, and it seemed as though we were about as far from Him as we could get. My marriage was in trouble, and my older son was showing signs of serious rebellion. As I look back, I realize that if my family and I weren't in the messes we were in at the time, I probably never would have turned to God the way I did. That day, I got on my knees and told the Lord that I was tired of being in control of my life, and I was handing it over to Him. I asked Him to transform me and my family, and to use us for His glory.

I suppose I was a bit shocked when I realized that my husband and my children were not thrilled when I surrendered my life to the Lord. What really hurt was that in some respects, they were downright hostile to my newfound faith. As I poured my heart out to God about it, He gave me the promise above to pray and claim for my loved ones. They certainly were believing the wrong things, as I had been, and I longed to see them accept instruction in the Word of God. The Living Bible translation says, "Those in error will believe the truth, and complainers will be willing to be taught!" (Isaiah 29:24 TLB) Every time I tried to save my family members from their error, and to minister truth to them, they complained and criticized me for it. So I reminded myself of this precious promise from God whenever I began to get discouraged.

As I persevered in faith, I saw my husband and both of my sons turn to the Lord with all their hearts. My older son, Joseph, started a Bible club in his high school that changed countless lives. And my younger son, John, launched one of the first and largest Christian music web sites in the world. My husband has graciously supported and financed my ministry all these years. And I'm so thankful that I didn't give up believing God for my family during those dark and difficult days.

You can't imagine the awesome ways that the Lord will bless and use you and your family, if you will claim this promise from His Word. Refuse to get discouraged or offended when they complain and criticize you for your faith. God will reward your faithfulness and your persistence, and the day will come when you will see your loved ones come into the Kingdom for all eternity!

Lord, I confess that it hurts me deeply when the people I care about criticize me for my devotion to You. I ask that You strengthen and comfort me so that I can stand firm in my faith, with joy in my heart. Prepare the hearts of my loved ones to be receptive to the truth that is spoken to them, both by me and by others. Today I choose to resist discouragement and despair, and to pray and claim Your promises of salvation and sanctification for all my family members! (Acts 16:31)

Promise-Power Point: As I pray and stand in faith for the salvation and deliverance of my loved ones, God will enable them to believe the truth.

Comfort and Joy

"I will turn their mourning into gladness; I will give them comfort and joy instead of sorrow." Jeremiah 31:13 NIV

Here is a personal promise from God that when we suffer loss or heartache of any kind, He will exchange our sorrow for His supernatural comfort and joy, if we look to Him. When my father suffered a fatal heart attack, and his death caught us all by surprise, I couldn't help thinking about all of the future events and blessings that he would miss out on. He would never meet my sons' future wives. He would never dance at their weddings. He would never experience the birth of his great-grandchildren. And he would never share another Christmas with us.

One of the things that my father left me with was a deep appreciation for Christmas. Even though he had a great sense of humor, Dad was mostly a very serious man, with a great burden for wanting to provide well for his large family. Even as a child, I could see the weight of this burden on my father's shoulders, and how hard he worked, especially during tax season.

After he served in the Air Force during World War II, he went to college to become an accountant, and he eventually became a CPA. I couldn't help noticing that everything my dad did was geared toward being a good provider for our family. At Christmas time, however, Dad became a different person. He sang more, he joked more, and he and my mom decked our house with cheery decorations from top to bottom. Christmas songs and hymns were always being played. And it's at Christmas time that I miss my dad the most.

After my father died, all along the way, God was there sustaining me with His comfort, and lifting me up with His joy. When my son, John, and his wife, Amy, announced that I would soon become a grandmother, they told me that if they had a son, they would name him William, after my dad. I attended William's birth, and I had the privilege of cutting his umbilical cord. And watching this precious child grow and learn and laugh fills me with more comfort and joy than I ever imagined.

No matter what you are going through today, God offers you His comfort and joy. Believe it, ask for it, and receive it with gratitude. It's one of the ways He proves that He loves you, and He cares.

Lord, whenever I am suffering or hurting somehow, please remind me of Your promise of comfort and joy. Speak to my heart and reassure me that no matter what I go through, You will be there to sustain me and lift me up. When I am tempted to dwell on my hurts and heartaches, surround me with believers who will encourage me with Your promises. Today, I choose to look to You for hope, healing, and strength!

Promise-Power Point: *I don't have to suffer in silence, or drown in despair, because God will fill me with His comfort and joy as I look to Him.*

God's Very Best

"If you are willing and obedient, you will eat the best from the land." Isaiah 1:19 NIV

When I discovered the promise above more than 20 years ago, it changed my life. Until that time, I had been a Christian, but I was not experiencing His best in any way. When I finally surrendered my life to the Lord, everything – and I mean everything – changed. It's one thing to be a Christian. It's another thing to be what I call a "surrendered" Christian. What's the difference? A Christian has a superficial, and therefore, mediocre relationship with God. He makes his own plans and decisions, apart from God and His leadership and wisdom, and then will ask the Lord to bless them. On the other hand, a surrendered Christian won't make plans or decisions without first asking for God's wisdom and will, with the intent of following the Lord's lead, wherever that might take him.

Every day, Christians get involved in relationships that are outside of God's will. Then they ask the Lord to bless these relationships, which are destined to end badly because God is not in them. I did this myself many years ago, before I met my husband, Joe. I was in a destructive relationship for 3 years before it came to an abrupt end, which affected me mentally and emotionally for years afterwards. That's one reason why it grieves my heart to see good Christian people making devastating choices in this area. Unfortunately, when their lives are shattered, many times they turn to God and say, "Why did You allow this to happen?" It never occurs to them that they are simply suffering the natural consequences of their own poor decisions.

Jesus said, "I do nothing without consulting the Father." (John 5:30 NLT) If the Son of God had to consult the Father for wisdom and guidance, don't you think that His followers should, too? All throughout the pages of the Bible, the Lord instructs us – even pleads with us – to consult Him before we take action. And I've learned that so-called "unimportant" decisions can actually be very important, when it comes to seeking godly direction in a matter.

Isaiah 1:19 tells us how to experience God's best in every area of our lives. We adopt and maintain a willing and obedient mind and heart. We get up every morning seeking the Lord's will for us for that day, and we practice seeking His direction on a moment-by-moment basis, with the intent to follow His lead. This is how we live our lives in total surrender to the Lord.

I have gotten to the point where I wouldn't dream of making any kind of decision without first consulting God with a willingness to obey. And I never miss spending time with Him daily, reading the Scriptures, and waiting for Him to speak to my heart through His Spirit and His Word. I've found that it is a lot harder to miss God's best when I'm seeking Him with an open Bible, as well as with an open mind and heart.

You are not going to come up with better plans for your life than God has in mind for you. Take it from someone who has learned the hard way – the Lord's way is best, and you can experience His best when you let Him have His way in your life.

Lord, forgive me for trying to live my own way, and do things my own way. Today, I surrender my life and my will to You, and I ask that You take control. Teach me how to seek Your wisdom and direction for every area of my life, and for every decision, whether big or small. I believe that You have special plans for my life, and I don't want to miss out on any of them. Guard me from a rebellious spirit, and give me a tender heart and a tender conscience. Thank You for helping me to fulfill my God-given purpose and potential!

Promise-Power Point: *If I seek God's will and direction with a willing and obedient heart and mind, I will experience His very best.*

The God of Increase

"And God will generously provide all you need. Then you will always have everything you need and plenty left over to share with others." 2 Corinthians 9:8 NLT

When my husband, Joe, was filling our car up with gas recently, I looked at the prices and inwardly groaned. As I had many times before, I began earnestly praying that God would cause gas prices to come down. Suddenly, I sensed the Lord speak to my heart that if I would spend as much time praying for increase as I did for prices to come down, I would witness Him meeting our needs more abundantly. I regularly claimed His promise which says that He will "liberally supply (fill to the full) [our] every need according to His riches in glory in Christ Jesus." (Philippians 4:19 AMP) But the Lord was challenging me to pray and believe Him for greater increase than ever before – not just so that Joe and I could pay our bills, but so that we could be a blessing to others, too.

God reminded me of a verse in Scripture that says: "You will be made rich in every way so that you can be generous on every occasion." And the Lord goes on to tell us why. "Your generosity will result in thanksgiving to God." (2 Corinthians 9:11 NIV) God wanted me to diligently pray for increase because my generosity toward others would draw them to Him, and cause them to give Him glory and praise. These days, I don't just pray for grocery prices to come down, but I pray that God will bless me so much that I will be able to buy groceries for others on a regular basis, without having to worry about the cost.

The Amplified translation of the promise above in Second Corinthians 9:8 reads: "And God is able to make all grace (every favor and earthly blessing) come to you in abundance, so that you may always and under all circumstances and whatever the need be self-sufficient [possessing enough to require no aid or support and furnished in abundance for every good work and charitable donation]." It's plain to see that our God is a God of increase. All through the Scriptures, we see Him blessing His people so that they can supply the needs of others, without it being a hardship for them. Yes, it's true that we are called to give sacrificially. But it's also true that we should believe and trust God for the rewards of our giving that He has promised.

Today, God is calling you to begin praying and believing Him for increase. Are you ready to begin claiming His promises with confidence?

Lord, forgive me for failing to pray specifically for a greater measure of Your blessings. Remind me that when I fail to obey You in this area, I am failing to do my part to be a blessing to others the way You planned. Show me which promises to pray and stand on for my increase. And deliver me from any doubt or unbelief that would hinder my faith in these matters. Today, I choose to believe that as I seek You first, and keep You first, You will supply everything I need, along with a surplus for others, too!

***Promise-Power Point:** As I believe and claim God's promises of increase, He will bless me more and more, so that I can be a greater blessing to others.*

God Will Work

"I will work, and who can hinder or reverse it?" Isaiah 43:13 AMP

Through my ministry, I often hear from people who have lost their jobs and are desperately searching for new ones. My heart goes out to them because my own husband, Joe, has gone through some periods of joblessness. Several years ago, when the company Joe was working for went out of business, he found himself eagerly combing the internet and newspapers for a new position. As the months went by with no real prospects, my husband began struggling with discouragement and low self-esteem. Because he was in his 50s, he was sure that his age was causing him to miss out on the best opportunities. He also believed that because his field of expertise was diminishing, he was losing his marketability.

As I thought about all of the reasons my husband gave for his inability to find a job, the Lord brought to my remembrance the promise above. Here, God was assuring me that no matter what the odds were against my husband, He was more than able to provide Joe with the perfect new job. So I decided to stretch my faith and ask God for some specifics. I asked Him to grant Joe a job near our home, so that he no longer had to travel out-of-state to work. I asked Him to provide my husband with a salary that would exceed his expectations. And I prayed that God would grant Joe a new job where he could really enjoy what he was doing. Some weeks later, the Lord granted my husband an interview with the company that pays the highest salaries in our area. The job opening they had was tailor made for Joe's skills, and the fact that he was older and had years of experience turned out to work in his favor. When the company offered my husband a job, and asked him what his salary requirements were, they insisted on paying him more. And hardly a day goes by that I don't thank God for providing my husband with a local job that he really enjoys.

Our God is an all-powerful God. When He goes to work on behalf of His people, no person on earth and no devil in hell can stand in His way. God wants to do a work in your heart, your life, and your circumstances. Call on Him. Trust in Him. And claim His promise as your own!

Lord, forgive me for the occasions You have wanted to work mightily on my behalf, and my lack of faith has shut the door to Your blessings. Open my eyes to the opportunities and solutions that surround me right now. Reveal Your will for me, and help me to follow Your lead. Thank You that as I keep my trust in You, and my eyes on You, You will work unhindered on my behalf!

Promise-Power Point: When I ask in faith for God to work on my behalf, nothing and no one can keep me from His best.

God's Healing Report

"Surely [Christ] has borne our griefs (sicknesses, weaknesses, and distresses) and carried our sorrows and pains...and with the stripes [that wounded] Him we are healed and made whole." Isaiah 53:4, 5 AMP

Years ago, I sought medical treatment for severe back pain from the doctor who was treating the governor of my state. This doctor told me that there was no known cure for my back problem, and that I would eventually end up in a wheel chair. Because this man was so highly regarded in his profession, I took him at his word. That is, until the Lord led me to Isaiah 53:1 (NKJV), which says: "Who has believed our report? And to whom has the arm of the Lord been revealed?"

Here, God revealed to me that He had a better report for me than my doctor did. He challenged me to meditate on the verses above which speak of the healing and wholeness that Jesus bought for His followers on Calvary. And He urged me to believe and claim these precious promises for my healing. As a result, decades later, my back gives me very little trouble, and I am living a healthy and active lifestyle.

Jesus wants to be your healer, too. Whether it's healing for your mind, body, emotions, or spirit – lay hold of the restoration and recovery He has for you today!

Lord, today I commit to You all of my healing needs. Heal me everywhere I hurt. Whenever I receive negative reports from doctors or others, remind me that You have a better report for me. Teach me how to meditate on, and believe, Your every Word, so that I never have to miss out on any of the good things You have for me. Right now, I declare with confidence and conviction, "With the stripes that wounded Jesus I am healed and made whole!"

Promise-Power Point: Whenever I receive negative reports, I can lay hold of the hope and healing that God promises for those who believe.

Exceedingly Abundantly

"Now to Him who is able to do exceedingly abundantly above all that we ask or think, according to the power that works in us, to Him be glory..." Ephesians 3:20 NKJV

When my husband, Joe, had open heart surgery to repair a faulty valve, he was out of work for many months. For the first few months, he received his full salary, but once those benefits ran out, all we had to live on was a fraction of his regular income. At one point, Joe came to me and told me solemnly that in two weeks, we would not be able to pay our bills. The look on his face troubled me. I knew it was not good for him to be anxious or apprehensive during his recovery, so I went straight to the Lord in prayer. I knew God must have foreseen our serious financial problems as a result of Joe's surgery, and I believed in my heart that He had a plan for our deliverance.

As I spent time alone with the Lord and claimed His promises of wisdom and provision, He reminded me that I had been earnestly praying for Him to supply us with a new car to replace our 24-year-old one. At first, I thought it would be crazy – and even presumptuous – to continue to ask God for a new vehicle when we could barely pay our bills. But then I sensed that the Lord was challenging me to believe Him for something extraordinary. So I began claiming the promise above for our situation.

The Amplified translation of this verse says that God is "able to [carry out His purpose and] do superabundantly, far over and above all that we [dare] ask or think [infinitely beyond our highest prayers, desires, thoughts, hopes, or dreams]." (Ephesians 3:20 AMP) Wasn't God able to provide us with a new vehicle in spite of our financial situation? My head said no, but my heart said yes – so I asked. Less than two weeks later, the Lord opened a door for us to pay off our bills, and to buy a brand new car.

I shudder to think where Joe and I would be right now if I hadn't believed God for His miraculous provision during that difficult time. And it saddens me to think that I have spent most of my life failing to ask, and expect, the Lord to do "exceedingly abundantly" in our times of need. I urge you to do some serious soul-searching of your own. Have you been living on crumbs of provision because of your lack of faith? God has so much more for you. Decide today to dig into His promises, and open the door to His boundless supply!

Lord, forgive me for the times You wanted to do something exceedingly abundantly above all I could ask or imagine, and I failed to come into agreement with You. Give me revelation from heaven to know when and how to ask for Your best in every situation and circumstance. Teach me how to feed on Your promises, and to claim them according to Your will and pleasure. Today, I choose to believe You – not just for the ordinary, but for the extraordinary!

Promise-Power Point: God is willing and able to exceed my highest expectations when I ask and believe with all my heart.

The Rewards of Forgiveness

"But when you are praying, first forgive anyone you are holding a grudge against, so that your Father in heaven will forgive your sins, too." Mark 11:25 NLT

Here is a promise that I took hold of twenty years ago that totally transformed my marriage. At the time, my husband, Joe, and I had already gone through many months of marriage counseling, but we were still having trouble getting along and living in peace. I was concerned about how our problems were affecting our two young sons, so when I committed my life to God, I sought His will and help for our family. That's when the Lord showed me that if I was really serious about pleasing Him in this area, I was going to have to take the initiative, and begin loving and treating my husband in a Christlike way.

When the Lord showed me the verse above, I confess that it initially made me cringe. I knew in my heart that I was holding a lot of grudges against Joe because of all the times he hurt me over the course of our marriage. God showed me that if I would let Joe "off the hook," He would deal with him in ways that would bring healing and peace to our relationship. It was hard work, and there were many times that I was tempted to quit and give up.

At first, my husband remained bitter even after I made the decision to forgive him, and I had to do the right thing for a very long time before I got the right results. But I leaned heavily on the Lord all the way, seeking Him daily for strength, comfort, and encouragement. And little by little, our relationship got better and better in every respect, and today we have a happy and healthy marriage.

The Amplified translation of Mark 11:25 reads: "And whenever you stand praying, if you have anything against anyone, forgive him and let it drop (leave it, let it go), in order that your Father Who is in heaven may also forgive you your [own] failings and shortcomings and let them drop." Those twenty years ago, one of the things that gave me the motivation to apply this verse to my life and marriage was that I didn't want anything to come between me and the Lord. In this passage, Jesus is teaching His disciples how to have mountain-moving faith, and how to get our prayers answered. I decided that my relationship with God, and my prayers, were just too important to me to hold grudges and remain unforgiving. So even today, twenty years later, I am doing my best to walk in forgiveness toward everyone. I can't do it without God's help, but I know that He will never ask me to do anything that He won't equip me to do. Who is it that the Lord is asking you to forgive today?

Lord, forgive me for the times I've had an unforgiving spirit. Please help me to understand how harmful my unforgiveness is to my relationship with You and other people. Teach me how to be quick to confess my sins to You in this area, and to receive the healing forgiveness You have for me. Today, I choose to let go of all the grudges I have against anyone, and to begin loving them with Your kind of love. Thank You that as a result, I will be able to pray with more power than ever before!

Promise-Power Point:** **When I choose to walk in forgiveness toward others, I can receive God's forgiveness, and enjoy the life-enriching relationships and prayer power He has for me!

Our Mighty Warrior

"The Lord is with me like a mighty warrior; so my persecutors will stumble and not prevail." Jeremiah 20:11 NIV

When an angry gang of neighborhood kids began attacking our home and family because I stopped allowing my children to associate with them, we used the law and the courts to try to get them to stop. After all of our attempts failed miserably, the police told us that our only hope was to catch these kids in the act. In exasperation, I surrendered the battle to the Lord, and began claiming the promise above.

One evening, my husband and our oldest son discovered one of the troublemakers attacking our house. They took off after the perpetrator in hot pursuit, and the boy stumbled so badly that my son, Joseph, was able to grab a hold of him and stop him in his tracks. We called the police, who said that we finally had an ironclad case against the guilty parties. As a result, all matters between us and our neighbors were peacefully resolved, without us even having to go to court.

If you are in a battle of your own, please know that the Lord wants to reveal Himself as your "Mighty Warrior". Entrust the battle to Him, and watch Him swiftly and soundly defeat your oppressors!

Lord, today I commit myself to You, along with all my battles. Teach me how to cooperate with Your battle plan, so that I can lay hold of the victory that I know You have in store for me. Guard me from the bitterness, resentment, and desire to retaliate that would rob me of Your best. Thank You for being my Warrior-King, and for not allowing my enemies to succeed against me!

Promise-Power Point: If I will commit my battles to the Lord, and follow His lead, He will reveal Himself to me and my oppressors as my personal Mighty Warrior.

No Regrets

"The Lord says, 'I will guide you along the best pathway for your life. I will advise you and watch over you.'" Psalm 32:8 NLT

When my husband, Joe, and I were dining at one of our favorite restaurants the other night, the owner came by to chat with us. He shared with us how he had heard a report about people who were near death, and what regrets they had. Apparently, the report really made an impression on this man, and as he talked, I thought about some regrets of my own.

My biggest regret is that I waited until I was almost 40 years old to get serious about my relationship with God. I had been raised as a Christian, and had gone to church for many years, but I never had a deeply personal relationship with the Lord. I had listened to sermons for years, and I could quote some Scriptures, but I hadn't been applying God's truth to my own life. It wasn't until I began diligently studying the Bible, and applying its principles, that I began to know God personally, and to experience the life-changing power of His Word.

The promise above in Psalm 32:8 was one of the first promises that I prayed and stood on when I first surrendered my life to the Lord. I still claim it to this day. The better I get to know God, the more I desperately desire His wisdom, advice, and direction. I don't just want to follow a good path, but I want to follow God's BEST path for my life. And I know that He wants that for me, too.

The verse that follows this promise says, "Do not be like a senseless horse or mule that needs a bit and bridle to keep it under control". (Psalm 32:9 NLT) This is God's plea to stop resisting His leadership, and to humble ourselves and follow Him every step of the way. And this is where a lot of Christians miss it. God offers us His best, but He won't force it on us. It's up to us to choose it for ourselves, and to walk in partnership with Him to see it come to pass.

Speaking of regrets, since I have done my best to follow where the Lord has led me these past 20 years, I have had very few regrets. Most of my regrets are from the years before I got serious about my relationship with God. Today, I ask you to contemplate your own regrets, and to let them lead you to the only One who can make them a thing of the past.

Lord, forgive me for the times You have tried to lead me along Your best pathway for my life, and I have resisted and rebelled. Give me a willing spirit, and a humble heart, and help me to believe that You always want what is best for me. When I'm tempted to act like a horse or mule, remind me of what it can cost me. Today, I choose to follow You wherever You lead me!

Promise-Power Point: I will experience God's best in every area of my life, as I let Him lead me along His perfect pathway.

God's Empowerment

"I have strength for all things in Christ Who empowers me [I am ready for anything and equal to anything through Him Who infuses inner strength into me; I am self-sufficient in Christ's sufficiency]." Philippians 4:13 AMP

When I finally surrendered my life to the Lord for real, I was almost 40 years old. By then, I had been friends with many people who were not God's best for me. Some of them had been my companions for decades. They had been my fellow students and my coworkers. They had danced at my wedding, and had rejoiced when I gave birth to my children.

Once I began diligently studying the Scriptures, as the Lord led me to, I discovered verses such as Second Timothy 2:22 (NLT), which says: "Enjoy the companionship of those who call on the Lord with pure hearts." I had to admit that even though my friends weren't bad people by the world's definition, they didn't have a true fear of God, and they weren't walking in obedience to Him. So I began distancing myself from them, leaning heavily on the Lord for His strength, comfort, and wisdom all the way. And you know what? Leaving my friends behind wasn't nearly as difficult or painful as I had feared.

The promise above in Philippians 4:13 reassures us that God will enable and equip us with His own divine power to do the hard things He calls us to do. The Living Bible says it this way: "I can do everything God asks me to with the help of Christ who gives me the strength and power." Whether you need to say goodbye to some friends or loved ones, or you need strength to radically change what you read, watch or listen to, the Lord's supernatural help is available to you as you pray for it, and expect it. God is not going to instruct you to do something hard and then say, "Good luck! You're on your own now. Just do the best you can!" No, He is a just God, and because of that, you can bet that when He asks something of you, He will be right there guiding and strengthening you all the way. What difficult things is He asking you to do right now?

Lord, thank You that Your Word promises that whatever You call me to do, You will equip and empower me to do. Show me what areas of my life You want me to focus on and deal with today. Take away my fear of doing hard things, and don't ever let me try to do things in my own strength. Remind me that when You ask me to make changes, it's always for my good and Your glory. Today I declare that I am ready for anything and equal to anything through Christ who strengthens me!

Promise-Power Point: Whatever God leads me to do, He will empower me to do with His own strength.

Hold Fast

"But the seed in the good soil, these are the ones who have heard the Word in an honest and good heart, and hold it fast, and bear fruit with perseverance." Luke 8:15 NASB

A young woman wrote me saying that she and her husband desperately wanted a child of their own, but she had failed to become pregnant after several years of trying. When she asked for prayer and some words of encouragement, I lifted her up to the Lord, and shared with her some promises related to child-bearing. One was Exodus 23:26, which says that she would not suffer miscarriage or infertility. Sometime later, I heard from her again, saying that she had finally become pregnant, but had lost the baby through miscarriage in her early months. She was heartbroken, and her faith had been badly shaken, even her faith in God's Word. After I prayed for her and asked the Lord how He would have me respond, I shared with her the promise above in Luke 8:15. Here, Jesus tells us that if we will "hold fast" to His Word and promises, and refuse to let go, we will eventually reap the fulfillment of those promises. This dear woman was greatly encouraged, deciding to pray and stand on God's promises to her once again, and today, she is the happy mother of a beautiful little boy.

The Message Bible translation of Luke 8:15 says: "But the seed in the good earth – these are the good-hearts who seize the Word and hold on no matter what, sticking with it until there's a harvest." There's a good reason why the Master told us to hold on to His Word no matter what. He knows that we have an enemy, Satan, who does not want us to experience God's best for our lives. In this lady's case, suppose she has a child who is destined by God to lead many lost people into a saving relationship with Christ? The devil is not going to want to take that chance, so he will do everything he can to thwart God's good plans. That's why, as Jesus says, whenever someone hears the Word, "Satan comes immediately and takes away the Word that was sown in their hearts." (Mark 4:15 NKJV) The devil will not be able to succeed, if we will heed the Lord's warning and persevere in holding fast to His promises.

If you believe that God has given you a promise, and it seems as though it will never come to pass, I urge you not to let go of His Word out of discouragement or despair. Remember Jesus' words of instruction and encouragement, and hold on until you reap the rewards He has in store for you!

Lord, forgive me for the times I failed to receive the fulfillment of Your promises because of my lack of faith. Grant me the patience and perseverance I need to lay hold of all the good things You have for me. Give me wisdom and discernment to know which promises are Your will for my life. Today, I choose to follow You wherever You lead, and to hold fast to Your promises until they come to pass!

Promise-Power Point:** **When I hold on to a promise that God has given me, refusing to let go in times of disappointment and despair, I will see the manifestation of that promise and reap all of its rewards.

Exploits for God

"The people who know their God shall be strong and carry out great exploits." Daniel 11:32 NKJV

When my older son, Joseph, felt led by God to start a Bible club in his public high school, not everyone was happy about it. Some of the students and faculty wanted the club to simply go away, and they often let my son know it. When the school refused to allow my son the same rights that were given to other school clubs, Joseph voiced his frustration and discouragement to me, and I sought the Lord for His will in the matter. I contacted a Christian legal organization that was familiar with students' rights where Bible clubs were concerned, and they offered to threaten my son's school with a lawsuit, if I would just say the word. They warned me that if I pursued this course of action, however, it could result in some negative consequences for my son.

I continued to seek God for His wisdom and direction, and I told my son exactly what our options were, along with their possible outcomes. Joseph was determined to take a stand against the school's persecution, so we went ahead with taking legal action. As soon as the school received the threat of a lawsuit on our behalf, they backed down and agreed to give the Bible club the same rights and privileges as all the other school clubs. And I am thankful to report that my son never experienced any significant retaliation as a result of his actions.

The Amplified translation of the promise above says: "The people who know their God shall prove themselves strong and shall stand firm and do exploits [for God]." (Daniel 11:32 AMP) When we decide to live our lives for God, and make getting to know Him our number one priority, He will strengthen us to stand firm against those things and people that get in the way of His perfect will. He will enable and empower us to "do exploits" for Him that will give Him great glory, and lead others to Him. Because my son took his stand against the school's attempt to bury his Bible club, he and his club went on to change hundreds of lives for the glory of God.

When people are inspired by my ministry, and they ask me how they can have a ministry of their own, I tell them simply, "Get to know God". The more personal and intimate your relationship is with the Lord, the greater He can, and will, use you to make a real difference in this world!

Lord, I want so much to have You use me to touch and change lives for Your glory. I want to know You in every way You can be known. Help me to draw closer to You each day through spiritual disciplines, such as prayer, Scripture reading, and meditation on Your Word. Today, I choose to follow Your will for my life, and I look forward to the exploits You will enable me to do as I am faithful to You!

Promise-Power Point: As I get to know God intimately, He will empower me to perform exploits in His name.

God Cares

"The Lord is good, a refuge in times of trouble. He cares for those who trust in Him." Nahum 1:7 NIV

This promise from God holds a special place in my heart. The Lord gave it to me the day that my husband, Joe, had a massive heart attack, and I was sitting in a hospital waiting room, waiting to hear some word on his condition. As I meditated on this promise, I felt God's peace flood every fiber of my being. I couldn't tell you that I knew without a doubt that my husband would be all right, but I can tell you sincerely that I knew that God was with us, and He would act on our behalf somehow.

That day, I learned just how true God is to His Word when He says that He "cares" for those who trust in Him. Every step of the way, He showed my husband and me that He was with us, and we were in His loving care. He masterfully orchestrated all the details of the events that preceded and followed my husband's heart attack. And He did it in such a way that no one could deny that He was actively involved in every moment of that entire ordeal.

As I prayed and trusted God for a miracle that day, He granted my husband a miraculous recovery that amazed everyone who saw it. What the Lord did for my husband and me, He will do for you – if you will lay claim to His promise, and cling to it with all your heart!

Lord, I'm so grateful to know that You are a good God, and You want to be my Refuge and Rescuer in times of trouble. Please give me a trusting heart, so that I can receive the kind of care from You that You long to give. May my faith in You and Your Word grow daily, as I seek You with all my heart!

Promise-Power Point: I will experience the Lord's supernatural care when I believe in His goodness and hope in His promise.

Build on the Rock

"Unless the LORD builds the house, the builders labor in vain. Unless the LORD watches over the city, the guards stand watch in vain." Psalm 127:1 NIV

Every winter, my husband, Joe, builds an enclosure around our covered patio to protect our ducks and their house. The year that Hurricane Sandy hit our area, the Lord led me to pray before the storm that He would equip and enable Joe to build our enclosure to His specifications. In previous years, there were times when even minor storms ripped a hole in the shelter my husband had built. Now that we were hearing frightening forecasts of winds of hurricane proportions headed our way, we wondered how our temporary enclosure would fare.

The morning after Hurricane Sandy hit our area, Joe and I awoke to find three large trees in our backyard completely uprooted. But the temporary shelter for our duck house didn't sustain a single rip, hole, or wrinkle. I sensed the Lord saying to my heart, "Do you see what a difference it makes when you ask for My help when you build something?" And He impressed upon me the importance of building my life, my marriage, and my family according to His instructions.

The negative aspect of the promise above shows us that our efforts to create something apart from God will be in vain, and that no amount of preparations or precautions will be able to keep us from harm, if the Lord Himself is not protecting us. The good news of this promise is that everything we build on a foundation of Christ will stand firm and succeed – not only here in this world, but in eternity as well.

Lord, I want to build my life, and do all of my work, according to Your specifications. I want my marriage and family to be built on Christ, the Rock. Teach me and my loved ones to live our lives under the shelter of Your protection, so that we will be spared from hurt and harm. May I never labor in vain, or forfeit the protection and provision You have for me!

Promise-Power Point: *When I build every area of my life according to God's instructions, I will enjoy His supernatural safety and success.*

Never Give Up

"So do not throw away your confidence; it will be richly rewarded. You need to persevere so that when you have done the will of God, you will receive what He has promised." Hebrews 10:35-36 NIV

While driving on the highway one day, I saw a billboard that said, "Never quit trying to quit". It was a message about quitting smoking, but it spoke to my heart in regard to some bad habits that I had been wrestling with for years. Suddenly, I declared out loud, "I will not be defeated, and I will not quit!" As soon as the words left my mouth, I sensed that something had "broken" in the spiritual realm, and I knew that this was my moment – the time to finally break free from the things that I knew were holding me back from God's best. Sure enough, the Lord opened my eyes to some new, Spirit-inspired strategies that would finally help me to overcome.

The promise above assures us that when we refuse to give up pursuing God's will for us, we've got some rewards coming. They may include freedom, wholeness, peace, and success. But they will be exactly the rewards that we need and desire most. The Lord didn't fill us with His Spirit so that we could live powerless and defeated lives. We could do that on our own, with no help from Him. But He gave us His Spirit to indwell us so that we could achieve hard things, even impossible things, so that we could stand out among the crowd and draw others to Him. Never give up! The rewards you reap will be more than worth it!

Lord, thank You for filling me with Your Spirit so that I could live for You, and become all You created me to be. Help me to cooperate with Your Spirit at all times, so that I can achieve great things for You, and reap the spiritual and earthly blessings You have in store for me. Today, I take my stand and declare, "I will not be defeated, and I will not quit!"

Promise-Power Point: *If I will refuse to give up or quit in my struggles to become all God created me to be, I will receive all the good things He promises in His Word.*

Don't Fail to Ask

"You don't have what you want because you don't ask God for it." James 4:2 NLT

When my husband, Joe, got a new job years ago, he was very unhappy with his new office. He had always had offices that were bright, cheery, and roomy, and this one was dark, dreary, and cramped. Besides that, he had to share his office with a coworker who made his life miserable. When I suggested to my husband that we ask the Lord to provide him with a new office of his own that he would really enjoy, he said that there was no way that could happen, because his boss had just informed their department that there was no money available for any "extras". Joe also told me that the company would have to make major renovations to his building, and there was simply no way they would do that now.

I thought that this was the perfect situation for me to claim the promise above on my husband's behalf. If he wasn't going to ask the Lord for a new and better office, then I would do it for him. Not too much later, Joe came home from work one day, describing how his company was making major renovations to his building, and how he was getting a new office that was twice the size of his old one, with an entire wall of windows. Not only that, but he wouldn't have to share it with anyone else.

This message is for you today, dear one. You have hopes, dreams, and desires that you have never discussed with the Lord. Why not ask Him in faith for those things that you've never asked Him for before – and watch Him go to work on your behalf!

Lord, forgive me for the times that You had blessings, opportunities, and rewards for me that I didn't have the faith or trust to ask You for. Fill me with revelation from heaven that will help me to know and understand just how much You want to bless me. Prompt me by Your Spirit to pray for those things that You want me to, in every situation and area of my life. Today, I declare that I refuse to do without the blessings You have for me!

Promise-Power Point: God will do things when I ask, that He won't do when I don't ask.

Fearless

"I sought the Lord, and He answered me; He delivered me from all my fears." Psalm 34:4 NIV

I have claimed the promise above when I have been in some of the scariest situations in my life, and God has never failed to honor it on my behalf. One such situation was when my husband, Joe, underwent open heart surgery. He was in the Intensive Care Unit of the hospital at the time, hooked up to more machines and tubes than I had ever seen. At one point, a team of nurses and doctors came into the room in order to remove Joe from the ventilator that was breathing for him. When their attempts failed because my husband could not breathe on his own, I began seeing mental images of him being on a ventilator for the rest of his life.

I promptly left the Intensive Care Unit and went out in the hospital hallway. I sought the Lord in prayer and claimed His promise, asking Him to deliver me from all my fears, so that I could pray effectively for Joe and those who were trying to help him. Then I rebuked the fear and declared out loud, "God has not given me a spirit of fear, but of power, love, and a sound mind!" based on God's promise in Second Timothy 1:7 (NKJV). Then I praised the Lord for making me fearless, and for healing my husband. The next time the hospital team tried to remove Joe from the ventilator, their efforts succeeded, and from then on, Joe's health steadily improved.

I have learned from situations like these that fear is downright dangerous. It causes us to lose our focus, and because of that, it severely affects our faith and our prayers. We simply can't afford to be paralyzed with fear when praying effective prayers is critical, especially in life-or-death situations. Don't put up with fear in your life. Claim God's promises so you can live the fearless life that He's called you to!

Lord, I know that fear is not of You, and that Satan tries to use it against me to make me ineffective and powerless. Help me to spend regular time in Your presence and in Your Word so that my faith will increase, and my fears will decrease. Teach me how to rebuke fear every time it comes against me, and to claim Your promises of deliverance. Today, I choose to walk in faith, and not in fear!

Promise-Power Point: *I can live a fearless life when I depend on God and His promises to keep me free from fear.*

Later and Greater

"And though your beginning was small, yet your latter end would greatly increase." Job 8:7 AMP

When I discovered this precious promise in the Bible, I was overjoyed. I had been a stay-at-home mom for more than twenty years, and I had never had a real career or vocation of my own. When I finally dedicated my life to the Lord, I asked Him to use me for His glory. He gave me the opportunity to minister to teens when my son, Joseph, began a Bible club in his public high school, and I became the official "club mom". Several years later, the Lord led me to begin writing devotional messages for my younger son, John's, Christian music web site. The following year, I started sending out weekly newsletters, building a list of subscribers. Eventually, a publisher offered to publish my devotionals in book form, and I was able to reach more people for Christ than ever before.

I got a late start where serving the Lord is concerned. I didn't get serious about my relationship with God until I was almost 40 years old. And I didn't publish my first book until I was almost 50. Maybe you think that you have missed out on God's wonderful plans for your life, or that you're too old to do something great for God.

Listen to me today, dear heart. You are never too old to commit your life to the Lord, and to begin experiencing the good plans He has for you. But don't waste another moment. Believe His promise that your later years can be even better than your former ones, and begin anew with Him!

Lord, forgive me for the years that I wasted living according to my own plans, instead of Yours. Right now, I offer You all that I am, and all that I have, and I ask that You put me to work in Your kingdom. Help me to serve You with wholehearted devotion all the rest of my days. And make my later years greater than my earlier ones in every way!

Promise-Power Point: *God can turn my small beginnings into great accomplishments, when I live for Him and look to Him for purpose and fulfillment.*

Every Disease

"The Lord will keep you free from every disease."
Deuteronomy 7:15 NIV

This promise is one that I have prayed and claimed for myself and my family for many years. Yet, one day, the Lord challenged me to claim it for a very specific affliction that I had been suffering from for decades. It was one of those ailments that the medical establishment had no cure for. And though I sought the help of doctors many times, they offered me very little relief or hope.

That day the Lord dealt with me, He highlighted the word "every" in this verse, and He dared me to claim it for this particular stubborn affliction. He told me that when His promises seem too astounding to believe, if I will think of faith as a choice, rather than an ability, I will witness Him moving mountains on my behalf.

As I look back now, years after my deliverance, I'm so grateful that the Lord challenged me that day, and that I didn't shy away from proving His promise. What illness or affliction would you like to be rescued from right now, if you knew that you could ask for, and receive, healing for it from the Lord?

Today, I encourage you to focus on the word "every" in this promise from God, and lay hold of the deliverance that is available to you through faith!

Lord, I confess that some of Your promises are so amazing, that they seem too good to be true. Today, I dare to believe that You want me healed and whole, and I apply this incredible promise to the specific areas of healing that I need right now. Thank You for rewarding my faith in You and Your Word!

Promise-Power Point: God will prove that He is willing and able to heal me of every disease, when I choose to take Him at His Word and receive my healing.

Speedy Works

"For He will finish the work and cut it short in righteousness, because the Lord will make a short work upon the earth." Romans 9:28 NKJV

Years ago, my husband, Joe, and I decided to move out-of-state for the sake of our children. We were living in an area that was steadily going downhill, and because of that, there were hundreds of homes for sale in and around our neighborhood. Our realtor told us not to expect a quick sale, but within the first few weeks, we signed a contract with a new buyer. We needed a new place to live right away, so we told a realtor in our new state to find us an affordable vacant home in move-in condition. We knew this would take a miracle from God, and we earnestly prayed for one.

When we lost a bid on the first house we tried to buy, our hearts were heavy with disappointment, and we began to consider less desirable options, such as moving to a hotel or an apartment, and putting our furniture and possessions into storage. I fell to my knees in prayer, and I pleaded with God to move supernaturally to provide us with the perfect new home without delay. Within the next few days, we found a beautiful house that was vacant, in move-in condition, and in a very desirable area. We found out later on that we were the talk of realtors for miles around when we were able to secure a mortgage, buy a new home, and move into it in only nine days.

If you are in a tight spot of your own today, as a child of God, you can claim the promise above, and expect the Lord to move mightily and speedily on your behalf. You don't have a moment to lose – begin asking and believing right now!

Lord, I thank You that You are able to make a "short work" of things that would normally take many days, weeks, or years. Whenever I need a speedy answer or assistance, remind me to turn to You first. Help me to cooperate with You in the process, and to keep my eyes on You so that I won't become fearful or anxious. Today, I lay hold of the speedy works You have in store for me!

Promise-Power Point: **When I am desperately in need of speedy assistance, I can turn to the Lord for help, knowing that He is able to supernaturally hasten the answers to my prayers.**

Good Mornings

"O Lord, be gracious to us; we long for You. Be our strength every morning, our salvation in time of distress." Isaiah 33:2 NIV

I have prayed this precious verse from the Scriptures almost every morning for many years. It is especially near and dear to me when I have to be up very early, after going to bed later than I should. Or, when I have to get myself up to keep an appointment that is especially challenging or unpleasant for me.

Our mornings are important. The attitude we adopt when we first wake up can set the stage for how our entire day will play out. If our faith is flagging, and we have a negative mindset, we can go through our day feeling gloomy and oppressed. Instead of finding something to be thankful for, we can minister discouragement and self-pity to ourselves. And we can forfeit the blessings the Lord has for us that day. On the other hand, if we wake up with a bright, positive, and thankful attitude, we will open the way for God to pour His strength, peace, and joy into us. And we can receive the saving help He has in store.

Tomorrow morning when you open your eyes, pray this promise. Embrace the day that the Lord has given you, and watch Him reveal His love and care for you in fresh new ways!

Lord, I long for Your presence, Your guidance, and Your grace. Teach me how to wake up with a positive and grateful attitude every day. Enable me to resist all discouragement, negativity, and self-pity. And help me to always get the proper rest. May I wake up each morning eager to face the day, and feeling totally energized in every fiber of my being!

Promise-Power Point: **I will experience God's strength and saving help when I pray His promise, and begin each day with a positive and grateful attitude.**

The Lion's Den

"And when Daniel was lifted from the den, no wound was found on him, because he had trusted in his God."
Daniel 6:23 NIV

When it was discovered that I had a blocked tear duct in one of my eyes, I had to have surgery to correct the problem. Unfortunately, the plastic tube that the surgeon inserted in my eyelid caused me to suffer a severe allergic reaction. As a result, the corner of my eye became an angry red color that made me look as though I had been beaten. I cried out to the Lord for help, and He led my doctor to remove the plastic tube, but the blood-red look remained. When I continued to appeal to the Lord for help and healing, He led me to the verse above.

Just as God did not allow Daniel to suffer any injury in the lion's den, He would not allow any wound to be found on my face because of my eye surgery, or anything associated with it. As I claimed His promise in faith, it filled me with a fresh sense of hope, and gave me great comfort when I needed it most. When I went back to the doctor for my follow-up appointment, even he was amazed at how quickly my wound had healed.

Maybe you've been in a lion's den of your own, and you have suffered physically, emotionally, or mentally. Take heart, dear one. Today, the Lord is telling you that He has seen what you have been going through, and He cares and will rescue you, just as He rescued Daniel and me. Trust Him as an act of your will, and know that in the end, no wound or injury shall be found on you!

Lord, I know that when You allow me to suffer a lion's den experience, You have a good purpose for it, and You will cause it to benefit me somehow. Today, I put my trust in You, and I lay claim to the protection, healing, and wholeness that You promise in Your Word!

Promise-Power Point: No matter what I go through, or how much I hurt, no wound will be found in me or on me, as I claim God's promise of healing and deliverance.

Divine Protection

"For He will give His angels [especial] charge over you to accompany and defend and preserve you in all your ways [of obedience and service]." Psalm 91:11 AMP

When my older son was in high school, he needed me to drive him to the library in a nearby town. I wasn't familiar with the area, and when I made a wrong turn and found myself lost in heavy traffic, I began yelling at my son for causing the situation in the first place. As I made a sudden turn without thinking, my car careened into another vehicle, causing an accident which involved the police.

Frankly, this incident left me bewildered and confused. Just before the mishap, I had prayed and claimed Psalm 91 for our protection, and I trusted the Lord to watch over us. When my emotions calmed down, and I questioned the Lord about it, He showed me that because I had allowed my anger to gain control over me, I had opened a door for the forces of evil to attack my family, and I had forfeited the divine protection that I had prayed for.

Ephesians 4:27 (TLB) says, "When you are angry you give a mighty foothold to the devil." My friend, don't ever estimate the destructive power of uncontrolled anger. As the promise above in Psalm 91:11 reveals, it is when we are walking in obedience before God that we have all the resources of heaven – including angelic protection – at our disposal. With the help of the Holy Spirit, you and I have the ability, and the obligation, to keep our anger under control at all times. It won't always be easy, but it will always be doable, with God's help.

I urge you to keep Satan and his dark forces out of your life, your family, and your ministry. And enjoy the divine protection and peace that will save you from hurt and harm!

Lord, grant me revelation from heaven that will help me to understand just how devastating uncontrolled emotions can be. Enable me to resist becoming easily angered, offended, and embittered. Help me to never forfeit Your mighty protection or provision because of sin in my life. Today, I choose to walk in forgiveness, love, and peace!

Promise-Power Point: *I will have God's supernatural protection when I control my emotions, and walk in obedience to Him.*

Saying Goodbye

"Truly I tell you," Jesus said to them, "no one who has left home or wife or brothers or sisters or parents or children for the sake of the kingdom of God will fail to receive many times as much in this age, and in the age to come eternal life." Luke 18:29-30 NIV

When I decided to get serious about my relationship with the Lord twenty years ago, I didn't have any friends who were true Christ followers. Because of that, God led me to leave them all behind. Though He sustained and supported me so well during the process that it wasn't nearly as painful or difficult as I had feared, I had to endure a long period of being friendless. During those many months, I devoted myself to getting to know the Lord in a deeply personal way. I claimed the promise above, and I prayed earnestly that God would reward my obedience by bringing godly, believing friends into my life. When He finally did, I discovered just how important and wonderful it is to have Spirit-led friends who will pray for me, encourage me, and counsel me in good times, as well as in bad.

Jesus said, "Simply put, if you're not willing to take what is dearest to you, whether plans or people, and kiss it good-bye, you can't be My disciple." (Luke 14:33

MSG) One reason why the Master calls us to leave many things and people behind is that He knows that they can hinder us from fulfilling our God-given purpose and potential. We can't always see how they are holding us back, so we need to continually ask the Lord what changes and sacrifices we need to make. As He promises us in Luke 18 above, the rewards are guaranteed by God Himself. And they will exceed our highest expectations. Remember this: You can't out-give God. Whatever He calls you to give up, He will multiply back to you many times over. Trust Him. He always wants what is best for You. He is your Great Rewarder!

Lord, forgive me for the times You wanted me to leave people or things behind, and I hesitated or refused because of fear or doubt. Please give me a trusting heart that will be quick to obey You and follow You wherever You lead. Show me what or who it is You want me to deal with at this time. Today, I choose to put my faith and hope in You, and to say goodbye to everything and everyone who might hinder me from becoming all You created me to be!

Promise-Power Point: When God calls me to give up people or things, He will multiply them back to me many times over.

Blessing-Filled Sleep

"It is vain for you to rise up early, to take rest late, to eat the bread of [anxious] toil--for He gives [blessings] to His beloved in sleep." Psalm 127:2 AMP

This is a powerful promise from the Lord to His beloved children. While the world scrambles and grasps for material goods and financial success, you and I can rest in the knowledge that as we live for the Lord, and follow His plans, He will provide for us even while we sleep.

In the early days of my ministry, I got very little rest. I woke up early every morning, and I went to bed late at night, just so that I could spend countless hours studying and writing, and ministering to others. Instead of being led by God's Spirit, I was being driven. Some of my motives were right, but others were wrong. I was not pleasing God, and I was doing myself harm. Eventually, I wore myself out. And my body began letting me know that it was headed for a breakdown if I didn't slow down.

When the Lord led me to this promise, I felt convicted. He wanted me to trust Him – to lead me, to provide for me, and to reward my efforts at just the right time. Since then, I have done my best to get up each day seeking the Lord for His plans for me on a moment-by-moment basis. And every night before I go to bed, I ask Him to shower me with His blessings as I enjoy a good night's sleep.

Proverbs 10:22 (NIV) says: "The blessing of the Lord brings wealth, without painful toil for it." God has plans to prosper you without you suffering under the weight of a painful workload. Are you ready and willing to follow Him?

Lord, forgive me for failing to trust You to prosper me and provide for me. Show me how to position myself so that I can receive Your gracious blessings even while I sleep. Strengthen my faith in You and Your desire to supply me with everything I will ever need. Thank You that You are not a stingy God, but You delight in showering Your children with abundant blessings of every kind!

Promise-Power Point: *If I will trust and follow God's plans for me, He will provide for me even while I sleep.*

From Tears to Joy

"Weeping may endure for a night, but joy comes in the morning." Psalm 30:5 NKJV

My husband, Joe, and I have been raising pet ducks for 14 years now, and every time we have lost one, it has grieved our hearts. When our 8-year-old Pekin, Lily, developed some laying problems, we took her to the vet, and cared tenderly for her at home. We had already lost two other female ducks to laying problems over the years, and we didn't want to lose Lily the same way. But after several weeks of doing our best for Lily in our home, she died.

Our male duck, Larry, had already lost two mates, and he took their deaths very hard. Both of his previous mates had died at the vet hospital, so he never had any closure in those cases, and he had suffered terribly as a result. This time, our vet instructed us to leave Lily's body beside Larry for a while, so that he could see for himself that she was gone. Seeing Lily's lifeless body was painful enough. But watching Larry stand faithfully by her side after she had died was almost too much to bear. I wondered if I would ever be able to get those harrowing images out of my mind and heart.

The promise above tells us that while the Lord will allow us to go through some painful times, He will not allow anything to rob us of our joy forever. The Message Bible translation of this promise says, "The nights of crying your eyes out give way to days of laughter." One reason for this is that our God has given us the gift of prayer. Even in the darkest and most difficult times, we can pray for the Lord's comfort, peace, and healing, knowing that He will always answer those prayers. Jesus said, "Ask, using My name, and you will receive, and your cup of joy will overflow." (John 16:24 TLB) In Jesus' name, we can ask for wisdom, guidance, grace, and all we need to keep moving ahead with joy into all that the Lord has for us. In every trial, He has a plan for our recovery and victory, and we will see it unfold before our eyes as we follow His lead.

The Lord didn't simply sustain us through that painful time with Lily and Larry. He comforted us and healed our broken hearts, and He gave us a fresh anointing of His joy. Perhaps you have seen and felt some painful things that have left you hurting and disheartened. Let me assure you that God has a plan for the restoration of your joy. Pray for it. Expect it. And watch God keep His promise to you!

Lord, I am so grateful that You are the God who sees. You know every tear that I cry, and every pain that I feel, and You care. When I go through painful experiences, help me to turn to You first. Teach me how to pray for Your peace, comfort, and healing, and guard me from despair. Today, I claim the joy and gladness that belong to me in Christ!

Promise-Power Point: Even in the most difficult times, weeping must ultimately give way to God's supernatural joy.

Our Heavenly Guard

"You guard all that is mine." Psalm 16:5 NLT

One of the things I love most about knowing and serving God is that when we commit ourselves to Him, He becomes committed to us. He cares about what we care about. And He looks out for our interests. Of course, in many cases, He expects us to partner with Him in order for us to experience the blessings of His protection and provision. One way we can do that is to pray and stand on His promises. Psalm 16:5 above is the perfect example. I have prayed and claimed this promise for myself and my family for years, and we have reaped its benefits many times.

One night while my husband, Joe, and I were asleep, someone tied an explosive device to our above-the-ground pool in an attempt to blow a hole in it. The thought of thousands of gallons of water flooding our property was more than enough to make me feel uneasy. When my husband called the police to report the incident, the officer who inspected the damage could not believe that the explosion did nothing more than create a small crater in the side of our pool. There was no doubt in my mind that the Lord had protected us from what could have been a terrible calamity, and I thanked and praised God for His protection.

Another scriptural promise that I hold dear says, "You will know that your home is safe. When you survey your possessions, nothing will be missing." (Job 5:24 NLT) This promise is one that I have counted on when storms have hit our area, or when my family and I have had to be away from home. I like the way the Living Bible says, "You need not worry about your home while you are gone." God has made it clear that He longs to be our Protector, and He will reveal Himself as such when we take Him at His Word.

Lord, thank You that You desire to guard all that is mine and my family's. Teach us to cooperate with you fully to that end, so that we never have to worry about anything that belongs to us. Help us to continually walk in wisdom so that we'll never foolishly put ourselves or our possessions at risk. We rejoice that You will bring to nothing every scheme and plan that would come against us!

Promise-Power Point: As we look to the Lord to protect what belongs to us, He will guard all that is ours.

World Changers for Christ

"Be diligent in these matters; give yourself wholly to them, so that everyone may see your progress. Watch your life and doctrine closely. Persevere in them, because if you do, you will save both yourself and your hearers." 1 Timothy 4:15-16 NIV

Here is a promise from God for all of us who have experienced the blessedness of coming to Christ, and who have an intense desire to see others do the same. The Lord first showed me this promise in the earliest days of my close walk with Him. I was praying fervently for my husband and children, because they had no personal relationship with God, and they had no idea how desperately they needed Him. The Lord promised me that if I would spend regular time in His presence, studying His Word, and renewing my mind to the truth, my prayers would have the power to bring salvation to the lost, healing to the sick, and freedom to those in bondage. God assured me that as I diligently applied His Word to my life, allowing it to transform my character and conduct, people would see Jesus in me, and they would know that He was real. So as I "persevered" in these things, God kept His promise and brought my husband and my children into the Kingdom.

The Living Bible translation says, "Keep a close watch on all you do and think. Stay true to what is right and God will bless you and use you to help others." (1 Timothy 4:16 TLB) There are people in your sphere of influence right now who may not be reached when you tell them about Jesus. But they may be convinced if you will SHOW them Jesus through your godly character.

One evening many years ago, I got a call from my teenage son saying that he had been in a car accident. He was unharmed, but his car was completely destroyed. God enabled me to respond to the unsettling news with a quiet calmness. I had visitors at the time, and one of them was an unsaved teen who no one had been able to reach with the Gospel message. I found out later that as a result of my Christlike response to my son's accident, this girl gave her life to Christ. Since then, I've often wondered, "What if I had reacted differently?" It was a powerful lesson on how important it is for us to exhibit Christlike character at all times.

God has ways of enabling you to be a world changer, but you must cooperate with His plans for your spiritual growth and transformation. Are you ready to make a real difference for God?

Lord, I rejoice that You want me to partner with You to save the lost of this world. Open my eyes to the people who are in my sphere of influence right now who need to know You. Lead me to diligently study Your Word, and to plant its transforming truths in my heart and mind. Help me to persevere in my efforts to walk like You and talk like You. Today, I choose to cooperate with You so that I can be a world changer for Christ!

Promise-Power Point: As I am diligent to become more like Jesus, others will see Him in me, and want to know Him, too.

Seeing Eyes

"Moses was one hundred and twenty years old when he died. His eyes were not dim nor his natural vigor diminished." Deuteronomy 34:7 NKJV

I recently heard from a dear lady who asked for prayer, saying that she was in danger of losing her eyesight, and that she suffered terribly from the fear of going blind. I shared with her the verse of Scripture above, and I told her that I had been confessing and claiming it for 20 years, and I encouraged her to do the same, trusting God for His protection and healing.

When I was growing up, my grandmother lived with us, and my family and I watched her go blind due to glaucoma. Needless to say, it left a deep impression on me. When I began digging into God's Word, I discovered that even though Moses lived to be 120 years old, he died with clear eyesight and all of his strength. I was overjoyed, and I knew that the Lord was prompting me to pray and stand on this verse as a personal promise from Him.

Recently, I went to see a new eye specialist, and after he gave me a long and thorough examination, he told me, "You will never have glaucoma!" I knew that this man's declaration was a word of encouragement from the Lord, and I gave Him all the thanks and praise.

As you and I live our lives here on this earth, it's so important that we don't mindlessly accept and receive every negative report we hear as truth. Even if the report is based on facts and scientific evidence, God wants us to turn to Him for His wisdom and perspective in the matter. Jesus said, "What is impossible from a human perspective is possible with God." (Luke 18:27 NLT) If we will believe and pray as though the God of the universe has the power to change even the most solid facts, we will witness Him doing the "impossible" on our behalf.

Jesus said, "It will be done just as you believed it would." (Matthew 8:13 NIV) Here is a powerful spiritual principle that can work negatively, as well as positively. That's why it's so important for us to believe God for good things. Don't believe every negative report you hear. Instead, take your questions straight to the Lord and ask Him, "What do You have to say about this, Lord? What is Your best for me in this?" Then follow His lead and receive the good things He has for you!

Lord, forgive me for the times that I passively accepted negative reports about myself or others. Help me to cooperate with You for the growing of my faith, so that I can believe You for all the good things You have in store. Remind me that being passive can open the door to the enemy to come in and "steal, kill, and destroy". (John 10:10) Today, I declare with confidence and conviction, "Blessed are my eyes for they see!"

Promise-Power Point: When I see with the eyes of faith, I can receive the good things God has for me, instead of the evil things the enemy plans.

Wisdom for Relationships

"He who trusts in his own heart is a fool, but he who walks wisely will be delivered." Proverbs 28:26 NASB

I once heard a godly man preach a sermon that helped give me a new perspective on relationships. He said: "If you hit me on the head with a brick, I'll forgive you. If you do it again, I'll forgive you a second time. But if you continue to do it, I'm going to keep my distance from you because of all the lumps on my head!"

This is a good illustration of a "toxic" relationship – that is, a relationship that is harmful to one or both people. I often hear from Christians who are in toxic relationships. They think that because Jesus told us to walk in love and forgiveness, it means that we should tolerate almost any kind of behavior – including destructive behavior – from others. When these toxic people are their own relatives, these misguided believers see themselves as trapped, and destined to suffer at the hands of their loved ones for the rest of their lives. As a result, these poor folks have become ineffective for God, and they are never able to fulfill their God-given purpose or potential.

Solomon warns us in Proverbs 28:26 that when we trust our own heart, instead of walking in godly wisdom, we become fools, and we will suffer for it. The prophet Jeremiah wrote, "The heart is deceitful above all things." (Jeremiah 17:9 NKJV) In other words, both of these wise men are trying to warn us that we can't trust our own heart. It will lead us astray, if we let it. Our heart will keep us close to people who appear to love us and want what is best for us, but who are selfish, manipulative, and looking out for their own interests, at our expense. Jesus said that some of these people would be members of our own household. (Matthew 10:34-36) And Satan will do his best to use these loved ones against us.

The apostle Paul wrote: "If it is possible, as far as it depends on you, live at peace with everyone." (Romans 12:18 NIV) Notice how Paul puts restrictions on our relationships by saying "if it is possible" and "as far as it depends on you". This is because there will be times when we will be in relationship with people who are impossible to please – people who are not led by God's Spirit, but by their own fleshly desires and self-interest. Being in relationship with people like these can carry a very high cost, because in order to keep them happy, we will have to sacrifice following God and His will for us.

Scripture warns, "Guard your heart above all else, for it determines the course of your life." (Proverbs 4:23 NLT) God gives you the responsibility of guarding your own heart. No one can do it for you. It's up to you to seek the Lord about all of your relationships, especially your closest ones. There may be some people in your life right now that God expects you to "love from a distance". Rest assured that if this is the case, He will give you all the courage and strength required to do what needs to be done.

Lord, reveal to me any people in my life right now who I need to begin distancing myself from – physically, emotionally, or both. Show me how to do it in ways that are pleasing to You. Help me to never trust in my own heart, but to always seek You for Your wisdom and will for all of my relationships. Teach me how to guard my heart, and to seek out healthy and godly relationships. Bring people into my life who will encourage my devotion to You. Today, I choose to obey You in my relationships, and to move on into the extraordinary plans You have for me!

Promise-Power Point: When I seek and follow God's will and wisdom for my relationships, I will be delivered and kept safe from the hurt and harm that toxic relationships can inflict on me.

Mountain Movers

"Assuredly, I say to you, if you have faith as a mustard seed, you will say to this mountain, 'Move from here to there,' and it will move; and nothing will be impossible for you." Matthew 17:20 NKJV

Before I began studying the Bible in earnest and finding out what belonged to me in Christ, I passively accepted every sickness, disease, and symptom that came my way. Once I discovered that the Lord had delegated His authority to His followers, I began to aggressively stand against attacks on my health. (Matthew 10:1)

Recently, one of my doctors told me that I had to stop taking a medication that I had been on for years. I tried explaining to her how awful I felt whenever I tried to discontinue it. Nevertheless, she insisted that it was doing me more harm than good, and she told me that I had to stop it right away. I promptly sought the Lord about it, and I shared my fears and misgivings with Him. He led me to the promise above in Matthew 17:20, and He instructed me to sharply rebuke every unpleasant symptom that arose once I stopped my meds. As I diligently followed the Lord's instructions, I was able to stop my medication with very few problems.

If you are a follower of Christ, then you are a mountain mover, and "nothing will be impossible for you," as you follow His will for you. If you doubt it, then you are living well below your privileges as a believer, and you need to spend more time in God's presence and His Word, so your mind can be renewed to the truth. Notice that Jesus said that even if your faith is only the size of a tiny mustard seed, you can SAY.... In other words, faith speaks. It speaks to sickness and disease. To poverty, debt, and lack. To fear and doubt. And to everything that is not God's best for you. What is the Lord challenging you to speak to today?

Lord, help me to dig into Your Word and discover all that I need to know about my authority in Christ. Teach me how to speak to those things that are not Your will for me. Fill me with a holy boldness that will enable me to lay hold of all the good things You have for me. Thank You that as I follow Your lead, nothing will be impossible for me!

Promise-Power Point: When I exercise my authority in Christ, God will enable me to move mountains for His glory.

Overcoming Power

"Three times I pleaded with the Lord to take it away from me. But He said to me, 'My grace is sufficient for you, for My power is made perfect in weakness.' Therefore I will boast all the more gladly about my weaknesses, so that Christ's power may rest on me. That is why, for Christ's sake, I delight in weaknesses, in insults, in hardships, in persecutions, in difficulties. For when I am weak, then I am strong." 2 Corinthians 12:8-10 NIV

Ten years ago, when my son, Joseph, and his wife, Miriam, decided to move thousands of miles away, my husband, Joe, and I were already struggling with disappointment and discouragement. My husband's company had closed its doors, and he was left unemployed with no prospects of a new job in sight. Only weeks after our son and his wife departed, my husband suffered a near-fatal heart attack. This latest blow was almost too much to bear, and I sought the Lord for His wisdom and comfort.

God led me to His precious promise in Second Corinthians above, and He reassured me that He would give me all the guidance and grace I would need to "bear my troubles manfully," as the Amplified translation says. (v. 9)

As I look back, I have to marvel at all the ways the Lord strengthened and encouraged us during those difficult times. As we kept our eyes on Him, and looked to Him for hope and help, He led us out of discouragement and despair, and He moved us forward into the new things He had for us. God granted Joe a speedy recovery from his heart attack. And He provided my husband with a wonderful new job. All along the way, the Lord fulfilled little desires of our hearts, which lifted our spirits and brought us closer to Him.

My son and his wife still live far away, and to this day, I have to depend heavily on God's grace to bear it manfully. I have learned that no matter what comes our way, if we will walk closely with the Lord through each day, and look to Him for His guidance and grace, He will not let us cower or cave. And by His Spirit, He will give us all the power we need to show the world that His love and mercy are boundless toward those who follow Him.

Lord, when I struggle with discouragement or despair, help me to turn to You for wisdom and strength. Give me Your perspective in the matters that threaten to overwhelm me. Remind me that You are prepared to give me all the supernatural enablement I need to persevere and overcome. I don't just want to exist, Lord. I want to live the joyfully abundant life You've called me to, no matter what comes my way. Today, I lay hold of the overcoming power that belongs to me in Christ!

Promise-Power Point: In difficult or painful times, if I will look to the Lord for His overcoming grace, He will empower and enable me to live a life of victory and joy.

Supernatural Revelation

"For nothing is secret that will not be revealed, nor anything hidden that will not be known and come to light." Luke 8:17 NKJV

The more we read the Scriptures, the more we realize and come to believe that God desires to impart revelation knowledge to His children. The verse above is one example of this truth. When I have needed wisdom for healing, for my finances, for my relationships – or for anything else – I have often claimed this promise and the rewards it holds. Solomon wrote, "Wisdom is supreme; therefore get wisdom. Though it cost all you have, get understanding." (Proverbs 4:7 NIV) When we are in a tense situation and we're not sure what the right thing to do is, the Bible says that we can turn to the Lord for wisdom, and He will provide it generously, as long as we're asking in faith. (James 1:5-6)

Just this morning, I was claiming Jesus' promise in Luke 8:17 (above), because I've been praying about a certain situation for months, seemingly without results. I asked the Lord, "Show me where I've been missing it in this situation. Grant me revelation from heaven so that I can receive Your absolute best." I know that God says in His Word, "My people are destroyed for lack of knowledge." (Hosea 4:6 NKJV) So I'm keenly aware of how we can miss out on the Lord's provision and protection when we fail to earnestly seek His wisdom for our situation.

The verse directly following Luke 8:17 says: "So take care how you listen; for whoever has, to him more shall be given; and whoever does not have, even what he thinks he has shall be taken away from him." (Luke 8:18 NASB) Here, Jesus is warning us to listen carefully when we seek divine wisdom and revelation. If we don't, Satan could very well succeed in stealing it from us before it does us any good. (Mark 4:15) Once we hear the Lord speak to us, it's up to us to apply that truth to our lives and our circumstances, so that we can gain the best outcome that He has prepared for us. As we do our part – seeking, listening, and applying – God will do His part – providing, protecting, and blessing. What situation are you facing right now that begs for godly wisdom?

Lord, when I have a need or a question of some sort, remind me to turn to You first. Teach me how to seek You for the revelation I need, and give me understanding along with Your wisdom. Grant me listening ears and a listening heart, and enable me to apply Your wisdom and direction to my life and my circumstances. Today, I declare that I will never be destroyed because I lack knowledge of You, Your Word, or Your will!

Promise-Power Point: God will reveal "secrets" and "hidden" things to me when I seek His wisdom and listen for His voice, with the intent to follow His will.

Strong in God

"Be strong in the Lord [be empowered through your union with Him]; draw your strength from Him [that strength which His boundless might provides]."
Ephesians 6:10 AMP

Before my first grandchild, William, was even born, I offered to help my son, John, and his wife, Amy, to care for him. So when Amy had to go back to work when Will was less than 3 months old, I began watching my grandson three days a week. I had already felt stretched fulfilling my roles as a wife, mother, and minister of the Gospel, so taking on a demanding schedule as the caretaker of an infant was far beyond my ability to handle. Each time I sought the Lord about it, He assured me that I was in His perfect will, and that if I leaned heavily upon Him every step of the way, He would give me all the strength I needed to do this new job well.

One of the promises that I have eagerly claimed the past two years I've been taking care of William is the one above from Ephesians 6:10. Here, the apostle Paul instructs us to continually draw on the supernatural strength that is available to us because of our union with Christ. How do we "draw" on this kind of strength, as Paul says? We spend unhurried, undistracted time alone with the Lord on a regular basis. We feed and feast on His Word. And we "pray without ceasing," as Paul teaches us in First Thessalonians 5:17 (NKJV). But we don't just have a one-way conversation with God. We also make the effort to listen for His gentle voice speaking to us, as we seek Him in our quiet times with Him. We can certainly speak to the Lord while we are "on the go". In fact, we need to do that if we're going to stay in constant communication with Him, the way we should. But we will probably be doing most of the talking during those times, so we have to set aside a time each day for the purpose of hearing from Him clearly. If we don't, we will never get to where we need to go, and we are destined to get off track, and out of His will.

Maybe you are dealing with a very demanding schedule of your own right now. I urge you to seek God's wisdom to find out if you are heading in the right direction, or if you are taking on responsibilities He never asked You to. The Lord will empower you to perform the duties and tasks that He assigns, but He is not obligated to strengthen you to do things that are outside of His will. He is more than willing to give you clear direction for your life. Are you ready to seek Him in earnest?

Lord, thank You for the incredible power that You offer me because of my faith in Christ. Teach me how to draw on Your power to live the life You've called me to, and to perform the work You've ordained for me. Show me if there's anything I'm doing right now that I need to stop doing. And reveal to me what things You want me to take on at this time. Today, I declare that there is nothing that You will ask me to do, that You won't empower me to do in Your strength!

Promise-Power Point: As I follow God's will, and draw on His strength for my God-given responsibilities and tasks, He will fill me with His own "boundless might".

Relief and Redress

"[The Lord] permitted no one to do them wrong; yes, He rebuked kings for their sakes." Psalm 105:15 NKJV

When my husband, Joe, and I purchased a used car from a local dealership, the car's engine blew up the first day that he drove it to work. Buying that car was a hardship for us, and we could not afford to pay for the costly repairs that would be necessary to get it back on the road. Joe and I suspected that there had been something wrong with the car when we bought it, and that the dealership had been aware of it. But we had no proof, so we took the matter to the Lord and asked Him to fight the battle on our behalf.

That's when God led me to begin claiming the promise above. If the Lord is willing to rebuke even kings on behalf of His people, then you can bet that He'll rebuke car dealers. And that's exactly what He did. I have no doubt that it was God who caused the dealership to offer us a free warranty on the car before we drove it off the lot, and we were able to use it as leverage to get them to pay for all of the expenses involved in getting the vehicle back on the road.

When you commit your life to the Lord, He becomes committed to making sure that no one oppresses or takes advantage of you. He's got a plan for your deliverance every time, and you will see it unfold as you commit your cause to Him.

Lord, You see what I'm going through, and You care when people do me wrong. I ask that You take up my cause, and right my wrongs, and help me to cooperate with You all the way. Guard me from taking matters into my own hands, and help me to put my trust in You. Today, I look to You to rebuke and reprove those who are against me!

***Promise-Power Point:* God will grant me relief and redress when I am wronged, rebuking even those in authority for my sake.**

Rewards for Service

"God is not unjust; He will not forget your work and the love you have shown Him as you have helped His people and continue to help them." Hebrews 6:10 NIV

I began claiming the promise above in the early days of my walk with God. At the time, my oldest son, Joseph, had just launched the first successful Bible Club at his public high school, and I had taken my place as the "club mom". Each week, I would supply those who attended the after-school meetings with beverages and snacks. I also drove home every student who didn't have a ride after the meetings were over. In addition, I would study the Scriptures diligently, putting together lessons that the kids could relate to and learn from. As I got to know the Lord and His Word better and better, I was able to minister to the students that I drove home each week. After Joseph graduated, my younger son, John, took over the leadership of the club, so my involvement with it lasted for years.

I enjoyed this ministry that the Lord had blessed me with, but it was extremely hard work. There were times when I was tempted to give up and quit, especially when the club's attendance was very low. I had to constantly remind myself that, just like Hebrews 6:10 says, God is a just God, and He was not about to forget my efforts, or let them go unrewarded. One of the rewards He gave me during those years was seeing the lives of so many students changed for all eternity. Some of those kids went into ministry, and many of them led countless others to Christ. I would never know just how many lives were impacted by that club, and my tireless efforts, until I got to heaven.

One of the rewards I valued most was God blessing me with a new ministry that would enable me to reach more people for Christ than ever before. I joined the staff of my son, John's, Christian music site, answering prayer requests, counseling people with the Word of God, and writing devotionals. This is the ministry that I have now, and like my former ministry, it is hard work. But hardly a day goes by that I don't claim Hebrews 6:10, expecting the Lord to continually reward me for my work and my devotion to Him. When the prophet Nehemiah was laboring diligently for God and His people, He prayed: "Remember, O my God, all that I have done for these people, and bless me for it." (Nehemiah 5:19 NLT) I have made this prayer my own many times, and I have seen firsthand how willing the Lord is to reward His children for their work on His behalf.

Whatever you are doing in the Lord's name today, especially for His own people, please know that He sees your efforts, and you have some rewards coming. They may be healings, material gains, new career opportunities, or new relationships. Expect them. Look for them. And remember to thank your faithful and gracious God when they come!

Lord, put me to work in Your Kingdom. Give me the strength and perseverance I need to perform and complete every assignment You give me. Guard me from discouragement and disappointment, and send fellow believers to minister to me when I need it most. Today, I choose to follow Your perfect plans for my life, and to reap the untold rewards You reserve for Your faithful ones!

Promise-Power Point: When I diligently carry out the assignments the Lord gives me, He will shower me with abundant and extraordinary rewards.

Our Heart's Desires

"Delight yourself in the Lord and He will give you the desires of your heart." Psalm 37:4 NIV

Since I've been walking closely with the Lord these past 20+ years, I have discovered time and time again how He loves to give us the desires of our hearts. When my 22-year-old car began breaking down in the worst possible places, I began pleading with the Lord to provide me with a more reliable one. He answered that prayer by causing my husband, Joe, to offer me his newer car. For the next two years, Joe drove that old vehicle to work every day without complaint, even though he had to endure a constant stream of ridicule from his coworkers.

When it was time to retire our old car for good, Joe began shopping for a new one. He did his homework and went to the auto dealership knowing exactly what he could afford, and what he wanted. The first time he called me from the dealership, he told me that he had driven the car he thought he wanted. When he described it, my heart sank. I had been believing God for three years for a particular car that was bigger and more stylish than the one that Joe was considering. I asked the Lord to intervene and make sure that Joe made the right choice. And I encouraged Joe to do the same, and to even consider waiting until the following day to make a decision.

I continued to pray that the Lord would not allow us to make a purchase that we would regret later on. And I asked Him to shut every door against our buying the wrong car. I also reminded God about the car that I had been believing Him for all along, knowing that He is often the One who puts certain desires in our hearts in the first place. I've discovered that He does this so that we can partner with Him to receive His best.

The next day, when Joe went back to the dealership, he found out that the car he drove the previous day, and all those like it, had been sold. He was sorely disappointed, and I tried to encourage him, saying that God must have had something better in mind for us. I earnestly prayed for God's favor upon my husband, and as it turned out, the dealership offered Joe the bigger, more stylish car that I wanted, for less money than the smaller one! Joe and I both knew that this was God's best for us, and now every time I get in that car with my husband, I thank and praise the Lord for giving me the desire of my heart – at an extraordinary price!

Perhaps you have a desire in your heart right now that seems out of reach for you. If you are living for the Lord, and finding your delight in Him, you don't have to settle for less than His very best. Ask Him for the desires of your heart today, believing with all your heart that He's a good God, and He loves to bless you abundantly!

Lord, teach me how to make You the delight of my life. Expand my vision so that I can believe You for the extraordinary things You have in store for me. Help me to never settle for less than Your best. And align my will with Yours so that I'll only have desires that please You. Today, I choose to cooperate with You to receive all the too-good-to-be-true blessings You have for me!

Promise-Power Point: When I live my life loving the Lord and delighting in Him, He will give me the desires of my heart, no matter how unlikely they may seem.

Declare and Establish Your Victory

> *"You shall also decide and decree a thing, and it shall be established for you; and the light [of God's favor] shall shine upon your ways." Job 22:28 AMP*

I can still remember the day when the Lord showed me the promise above for the first time. It was as if He had handed me a gift – a gift that would enable me to turn defeat into victory, by speaking words of faith. Since then, whenever bad news has come my way, I have claimed this promise, and used it as a weapon against Satan and the forces of hell.

One time in particular was when my husband, Joe, was suffering terribly from a large growth in his neck. After going through medical tests, and being examined by doctors, Joe was told that there was a 90 percent chance that he had cancer. At first, fear hit me like a ton of bricks. But then I spent some time in prayer and Scripture reading, seeking the Lord's perspective in the matter. He showed me that if I passively accepted Joe's diagnosis, it would "be established," and there would be little hope for my husband. But if on the basis of Job 22:28, I declared and decreed that Joe was healed and free from cancer and disease, I would see God move mightily on our behalf.

From that time on, I declared God's promises of healing and deliverance for my husband. Two more doctors, and more tests, confirmed that Joe most likely had cancer. Still, I continued to decree that Joe was cancer free, and that any growth in his neck had to leave immediately and forever. Finally, the day came when Joe was to go to the hospital to have the growth in his neck biopsied. As the doctor probed and searched for that growth, it was nowhere to be found. The same tests that confirmed the presence of the growth now confirmed its absence. The doctors couldn't explain it, but they don't have to. Joe and I know in our hearts that God worked a miracle because we trusted in His promises, instead of the medical reports.

When trouble comes your way, don't just passively accept your circumstances. Get God's perspective in the matter, declaring and decreeing His will for you – and watch Him do what only He can do!

Lord, when the odds are stacked against me, help me to turn to You first. Show me how to cooperate with You so that the odds can be turned in my favor. Teach me how to declare and decree Your will, Your Word, and Your promises in the face of destruction and defeat. Today, I choose to believe and declare that with You on my side, nothing and no one can keep me down!

Promise-Power Point: *If I will refuse to respond to my troubles passively, and seek God's perfect plans for me, I can declare my victory and see it come to pass.*

Perfect Peace

"You will keep him in perfect peace whose mind is stayed on You, because he trusts in You." Isaiah 26:3 NKJV

If you are in need of God's peace today, then this is the promise for you. It's the Lord's personal guarantee that when we keep our minds and thoughts fixed on Him, and put our trust in Him, He will fill us with His "perfect peace". You can't get any better than perfect when you're talking about peace. And only God Himself can make a promise like this.

We live in a scary world. Jesus knew this, and that's why before He went to the cross, He gifted us with His own matchless peace. (John 14:27) The promise above from Isaiah tells us a couple of ways we can hold on to our peace at all times. First, we need to keep our minds, or "thoughts" (NLT), "stayed" on God. Not on ourselves, our limitations, or inadequacies. Not on our circumstances or other people. But on God. Our minds will keep trying to drift away from focusing on the Lord, but we have the power to discipline our thoughts, and we can purposefully draw them back to Him. As we meditate on God and His unlimited power, wisdom, and love, negative thoughts and emotions will flee, and they will be replaced by the perfect peace that He promises.

Second, we must make a quality decision to trust God. Trust is something that can be properly placed, or misplaced. We direct it ourselves, and no one can do it for us. As we make a conscious choice to put our trust in the Lord, He rewards our faith by filling us with His own brand of peace that causes fear and doubt to evaporate.

I have heard my husband, Joe, relate the events of his heart attack many times, and each time, he tells people how I was standing across from his hospital bed in the emergency room with a smile on my face, while doctors and nurses labored to save his life. I often wonder if people mistakenly think that I didn't care that my husband almost died, or that I didn't understand the gravity of the situation. The truth is that I was well aware of the threat to my husband's life, and that's exactly why I had committed Joe and the situation to God, and had put my trust in Him and His promises. And as a result, I experienced His indescribable peace.

The Amplified Bible translation of Isaiah 26:3 reads: "You will guard him and keep him in perfect and constant peace whose mind [both its inclination and its character] is stayed on You, because he commits himself to You, leans on You, and hopes confidently in You." If you are a follower of Christ, then you have the capacity to enjoy God's supernatural peace in any and every circumstance. Commit yourself to Him, lean on Him, and put your hope in Him. When you do, you have God's personal guarantee that His own unshakable peace will sustain you.

Lord, I rejoice that You want me to live in peace, no matter what is going on in my life or around me. Help me to cooperate with You for the building of my faith, so that I can learn to resist all fear and doubt that come against me. Teach me how to discipline my thoughts, so that they won't be able to torment me. Today, I choose to put my trust in You, and keep my mind on You, so that I can reap the harvest of peace You have for me!

Promise-Power Point: *I will experience God's perfect peace when I place my trust in Him, and focus my thoughts on Him.*

Superhuman Energy

"For this I labor [unto weariness], striving with all the superhuman energy which He so mightily enkindles and works within me." Colossians 1:29 AMP

Did you know that as a follower of Christ, the Lord has promised you "superhuman energy" when you need it? It's true. And it's not just for ministry duties, but it's for anything the Lord has called us to do. In my case, in addition to my responsibilities as a wife, mother, and minister of the Gospel, God has called me to care for my grandson, William, on days when his parents have to work. In my son, John's, case, he owns and operates one of the largest and most popular Christian music web sites today. And in my daughter-in-law, Amy's, case, she works as an operating room nurse in a local hospital. Both are very demanding jobs, so I have committed myself to taking care of their son, William, on days when they have to work.

I raised my own two sons when I was very young, and even then it was extremely difficult at times. Now that I'm over 60 years old, and I've been helping to raise my grandson since he was an infant, I have needed more than normal human strength – I have needed superhuman strength, especially if I want to do the job well. Because of that, I have to claim God's promises of supernatural energy every day, and the promise above is the perfect example.

How do you know if you are operating in God's strength, instead of your own? There is a "flow" to your efforts. It can still be a struggle at times, and you can still feel exhausted at the end of the day, but there is no harm to your health, and you are able to keep going. This kind of divine energy cannot be experienced apart from having a close relationship with God. In fact, it flows out of our union with Christ, and it keeps flowing as we seek His presence and His ways day by day. Having His Word abiding in us, as well, can enable us to tap into even more heavenly resources for our work. More energy, more wisdom, and more skill.

Whatever God has called you to do, He is more than willing to equip you for the job. Ask Him to teach you how to lean heavily on Him, and to learn from Him, so that you can not only do your work well, but do it with a holy ease and joy!

Lord, thank You for Your promise of superhuman energy to do the work You've called me to do. Help me to know You in a deeper way each day. Teach me how to cling to You and Your promises, so that I can accomplish all of my divine assignments without harming my health or losing my joy. Today, I choose to leave my self-dependency behind, and to work and live my life relying on You and Your incomparable power!

Promise-Power Point: God will equip me with superhuman energy to accomplish my assignments from Him, if I will walk closely with Him, and lean heavily upon Him.

Closed Doors

"In the days to come you will understand all this."
Jeremiah 30:24 NLT

After my husband, Joe, and I were married for about a year, I quit my high-pressure office job to find something less stressful. I had always interviewed well, and I was accustomed to being hired on the spot, but this time, no one would hire me. In one case, a company interviewed me and gave me a challenging test. Afterwards, the man in charge told me that I had scored higher than anyone else they had ever tested. To my surprise, he refused to hire me. As I shared my discouragement and bewilderment with my husband, he convinced me that it was time for us to begin raising a family. Years later, I found out that all along, I had a health condition that could eventually rob me of my ability to have children, and I thank God that He forced me to put my career on hold.

To this day, the Lord often brings to mind the promise above, and the experience I just mentioned, whenever He closes a door that causes me disappointment or confusion. It's His way of saying, "You don't understand what I'm doing right now, but in the days to come, you will. Just believe that I love you and want what's best for you."

When our sons were very young, an accounting position opened up at my husband's workplace, and we both earnestly prayed that he would get the job. Joe had gone back to school after we got married, so that he could get a degree in accounting, and increase his earning potential. With me being a stay-at-home mother, and our family growing, we felt this new opportunity was an answer to our prayers. But when it came time to fill the position, Joe was passed over for someone else. It wasn't until a year later, when the entire accounting department was eliminated from Joe's company, that we understood why God had closed the door on that opportunity.

Perhaps you are wondering what God is up to in your life right now, and you're feeling confused and forsaken. I believe that His message to you today is that He is up to something good, and He wants you to trust Him. If you listen very carefully, you just might hear Him saying to you, "In the days to come, you will understand..."

Lord, forgive me for doubting You when I sense that You are closing doors, instead of opening them for me. Help me to cooperate with You for the building of my faith. Remind me that when You say 'no' to a relationship, job, or opportunity of some sort, it means that You have something better in store for me. Today, I choose to put my trust in You, and to believe that the best is yet to come!

Promise-Power Point: When God closes a door, I will see Him open an even better one, if I will trust Him and refuse to doubt His goodness.

Peaceful Dwellings

"My people will live in peaceful dwelling places, in secure homes, in undisturbed places of rest." Isaiah 32:18 NIV

The Lord gave me this promise when my family and I were having some serious problems with our neighbors. My husband, Joe, and I had discovered that some of the neighborhood kids that our sons were playing with were negative influences on our children. So when we put a stop to our boys playing with them, war broke out, and we started experiencing severe attacks on our home and property. We took our neighbors to court twice, but that only made the problem worse. The attacks on our home resulted in so much damage, that we eventually had to replace all of the siding on our house.

When the Lord gave me the promise above, I prayed it and stood on it for our deliverance daily. When months passed by and we still suffered attacks from our neighbors, I held on to this Word from God, trusting Him to act on our behalf. One day, as I was praying and claiming this promise, I realized that the attacks had stopped. The Lord did come to our rescue, and He did make our surroundings peaceful, secure, and undisturbed.

Maybe you are having neighbor troubles of your own today. If so, I understand your anguish, and my heart goes out to you. Let me encourage you not to give up hope. God sees your problem, and He wants to help. Do your part by claiming His promise of deliverance, as I did, and watch Him do His part to rescue and vindicate you!

Lord, grant me and my family a peaceful home and peaceful surroundings. You are the Prince of Peace, and nothing is too difficult for You. Today, I put my hope in You and Your Word, and I look forward to the peace, security, and rest that the fulfillment of Your promise will bring!

Promise-Power Point: As I seek God and His plan for my deliverance from neighborhood problems, I will experience the peaceful home and surroundings that He promises in His Word.

Sow His Promises

"Those who sow in tears will reap with songs of joy. He who goes out weeping, carrying seed to sow, will return with songs of joy, carrying sheaves with him."
Psalm 126:5-6 NIV

The Lord gave me this promise many years ago, when I was going through a particularly dark and painful time. He showed me that when I am hurting somehow, or when I have a need of some kind, if I will ask Him for a promise of hope for my situation – and hold on to it throughout my trial – He will reward me with the fulfillment of that promise. Jesus called God's Word "seed" in Luke 8:11, and in Luke 8:15, He said that those who hold fast to the Word will eventually bear fruit, if they persevere.

Over the years, I have seen the Lord fulfill His promises to me in some of the most "hopeless" cases you can imagine. Sometimes, I didn't have to cling to His promise for very long at all before the answer came. Other times, I had to claim His promise for many months or even years. But looking back, I can honestly say that every single time, it was more than worth it. Frankly, I have never seen God work as mightily in situations as He does when His children are hanging on to His promises. The Lord loves when we take Him at His Word, and trust in His faithfulness.

The Message Bible translation of the promise above reads: "Those who planted their crops in despair will shout hurrahs at the harvest; those who went off with heavy hearts will come home laughing, with armloads of blessing!" (Psalm 126:5-6 MSG) If you are a child of God, then He has some special promises for you that He is longing for you to claim right now. Seek Him in His Word, plant your seed of promise, and expect a harvest of blessings in return!

Lord, I rejoice that in every situation I will ever face, You have promises of hope and victory that apply to my particular need. Teach me how to search out Your promises, and show me which ones You want me to lay hold of. Thank You for giving me the faith and the perseverance I need to reap the harvest of blessings You have for me!

Promise-Power Point: When I sow God's Word of promise through my tears, He will faithfully reward me with a harvest of miracle blessings.

A Quick Recovery

"Your recovery will speedily spring forth." Isaiah 58:8 NASB

When I discovered that I needed to have a medical procedure that could take weeks to recover from, I appealed to the Lord for His wisdom and help. I was caring for my grandson, William, on days when my son and his wife had to work, and I simply couldn't afford to take time off. The Lord showed me the promise above during my quiet time with Him, and He challenged me to claim it in faith for my recovery. He wasn't just saying that I would recover. He was telling me that He would supernaturally speed up the recovery process, as I chose to believe and apply His promise. As I took God at His Word, I was able to return to caring for my grandson very quickly, and I rejoiced in how the Lord delights in fulfilling His promises to us when we put our trust in Him.

Maybe you are in need of a recovery of your own today. Perhaps you need a recovery in your finances. Or maybe you need to recover from a very deep emotional pain. You may even need a spiritual recovery, if you have allowed yourself to drift away from God and His perfect plans for you.

Whatever kind of recovery you are in need of today, please know that God sees your need and feels your pain. Reach out to Him in heartfelt prayer right now, and claim the supernatural hope and healing that belong to those who believe!

Lord, I desperately need a touch from You today. I am hurting in ways that I can't even describe, and I ask that You grant me the kind of healing that can only come by Your hand. Thank You that as I keep my eyes on You and Your promise, my recovery will "speedily spring forth"!

***Promise-Power Point:** I can receive supernatural recovery in every area of my life when I believe God's promise, and look to Him to keep His Word.*

Unfamiliar Paths

"I will lead the blind by ways they have not known, along unfamiliar paths I will guide them; I will turn the darkness into light before them and make the rough places smooth. These are the things I will do; I will not forsake them." Isaiah 42:16 NIV

God gave me this promise when I was seeking Him about overcoming some bad habits that I had wrestled with for years. It wasn't that I hadn't tried my best to get free, because I had many times. I had prayed every which way I knew how to pray, but I kept failing time and time again. By the time I read this verse in a fresh new way, I had so many failures behind me that I couldn't focus on anything else.

Here, the Lord promises that when we see no way out of our troubles and heartaches, He will lead us along paths we have never before traveled, and He will personally guide us all the way. He will give us new ideas and new strategies that we've never even thought of before. They may be simple ones, but because they are directed by God, they will make all the difference. And when the process gets too difficult for us, He will smooth out the path ahead of us, and light our way, so that we can reach our goal.

If you are in a difficult place today, the Lord has a plan for your deliverance. Trust Him. Seek Him. Make His plans yours. And watch Him do what only He can do!

Lord, sometimes I can't see a way out of my pain and my problems, and all I can see are my failures from the past. Lead me along new and different paths now — paths that lead to the freedom and healing that I know You have for me. Today, I choose to resist feelings of failure and defeat, and I look to You and Your perfect plans for me!

Promise-Power Point: ***Even if I have failed many times before, God has a plan for my victory and success, and I will see it unfold as I seek Him and follow His lead.***

Doom the Devourer

"And I will rebuke the devourer [insects and plagues] for your sakes and he shall not destroy the fruits of your ground, neither shall your vine drop its fruit before the time in the field, says the Lord of hosts." Malachi 3:11 AMP

If you read the verses preceding the promise above, you discover that when God's people give as the Lord leads, He is committed to protecting what belongs to us. I have claimed this promise in simple matters such as the welfare of my husband's garden. I have also claimed it when I or my loved ones have been seriously threatened in some way.

What the Lord showed me years ago is that the "devourer" can not only be insects or pests, but it can be any form of sickness, disease, infirmity, or pain. It can be accidents, injuries, or calamities. Or poverty, debt, or lack. Or theft or loss of any kind. Anything that would come against us to devour our bodies, our loved ones, or our resources is something we can claim this promise of deliverance for.

If you have not been claiming this promise for yourself and your family, then you are living well below your privileges as a follower of Christ. It's my hope that when you read this, you will promptly remedy that situation, and begin making the most of your glorious inheritance in Christ!

Lord, teach me how to give of my time, my talents, and my treasure as Your Spirit leads. Make me sensitive to the needs of others, and make me quick to obey You in this area. Help me to reap the fullness of Your blessings in Malachi 3:11 from now on. Thank You for rebuking the devourer for my sake as I live and give for You!

Promise-Power Point: God is willing to rebuke everything that threatens to harm or devour me or my family and He will do it when I hold Him to His Word.

Skills Blessed by God

"Bless all his skills, O Lord, and be pleased with the work of his hands." Deuteronomy 33:11 NIV

This is a prayer-promise that I stand on almost every day for myself and my loved ones. When I get into my car, I pray, "Bless all my driving skills, O Lord, and be pleased with the work of my hands." I want God's help to make me a safe, skillful, and responsible driver, especially when I have passengers in my car. I also pray and apply this promise to my writing and ministry skills. I not only want the Lord to give me supernatural skills, but I also want to speak and write in ways that please Him most.

When my sister was having the front steps of her house completely reconstructed, she was understandably concerned, and she asked for my prayers. I shared with her the scriptural prayer above, and I encouraged her to pray it on behalf of the men who would be doing the work on her house. She did exactly that, and when I saw her new front steps, I was amazed at the extraordinary skills and efforts that must have been involved to produce such beautiful results.

The Scriptures make it clear that God wants us to ask Him to be involved in all our efforts, not just so that they will succeed, but so that they will please and glorify Him. Proverbs 3:4-6 (TLB) reads: "Trust the Lord completely; don't ever trust yourself. In everything you do, put God first, and He will direct you, and crown your efforts with success." I know from experience that this promise can be applied to everything we do, including our food preparation. I am "famous" for my manicotti, my deviled eggs, and my apple crumb pie because before I begin them, I pray and claim this promise as my own, trusting the Lord to guide and bless my efforts. And I believe that it honors Him when others are blessed by my culinary skills.

When God created you, He gave you skills and gifts that are unlike anyone else's. He not only wants you to ask Him what they are, but He also wants you to seek Him for His divine blessing upon them. When you do, you will touch the lives of others, and give Him great glory!

Lord, reveal to me the special gifts and skills that You have blessed me with. Show me how to do my part to perfect them and make them more valuable all the time. I want to use them for the good of others, Lord, as well as for Your glory. Today, I choose to invite You into all of my work, and to seek Your blessing on all that I do!

Promise-Power Point: When I commit my work to God, and ask for His guidance and blessing, He will cause my efforts to succeed and prosper in ways that honor Him most.

Forget the Crisis Prayers

"I'm not going to listen to a single syllable of their crisis-prayers." Jeremiah 11:14 MSG

I was raised in a Christian household, and had been praying almost since the day I had learned how to talk. But if I were to be completely honest, I'd have to say that I did most of my praying when I was in trouble, and very little praying otherwise. In other words, most of my prayer time was spent praying what the Bible calls "crisis-prayers". The prophet Jeremiah gives an account of a period in Israel's history when God's people were not wholly devoted to Him, and He only heard from them when they were in distress. The Lord tells Jeremiah, "I'm not going to listen to a single syllable of their crisis-prayers." (Jeremiah 11:14 MSG) It saddens me every time I read this verse, because it reminds me of how shallow a relationship I used to have with the Lord myself. As I look back, I realize now why my prayers were, for the most part, anemic and powerless.

When I made a quality decision to get serious about my relationship with God, just before my 40th birthday, I began studying the Scriptures in-depth, having an intense desire to know Him in every way that He could be known. That's when I discovered that our God desires to have a deeply personal relationship with His children, and He expects them to love Him, seek Him, and serve Him with wholehearted devotion. When we make this kind of commitment to the Lord, one of the blessings we receive in return is the privilege of getting "ready answers" to our prayers. Jesus said: "If you abide in Me, and My words abide in you, you will ask what you desire, and it shall be done for you." (John 15:7 NKJV) One of the reasons why many believers today are not hearing clearly and consistently from God is that they are not "abiding" in Him. Abiding in Christ means that we give Him the best of our time and energy each day. He is the first one we think of and speak to each morning. He is the One we consult about everything, and the One who gets to have the final say in all of our decisions and choices. And He and His Word have first place in our lives.

Don't be the kind of believer who only prays "crisis-prayers" and gets sorry results. God has so much more for you than that, and He will share it with you if you give Him your best. Right now, make the decision to abide in Him all the rest of your days, and watch what He will do in and through your prayer life!

Lord, forgive me for the times that I failed to serve You with wholehearted devotion. Work in my heart so that I can begin loving You, seeking You, and serving You the way You desire and deserve. Don't let me settle for a lukewarm relationship with You. Fill me with a growing passion for Your presence and Your Word. Today, I commit to cooperating with You so that I can know You in every way that You can be known!

Promise-Power Point: *When I refuse to have a shallow relationship with Christ, and shun "crisis-prayers," I will experience a prayer life that will bring salvation, deliverance, and healing to countless people for the glory of God.*

Freedom and Healing

"Now the Lord is the Spirit, and where the Spirit of the Lord is, there is freedom." 2 Corinthians 3:17 NIV

Many years ago, before I met my husband, Joe, I was involved in a very unhealthy relationship that ended badly. It was such a negative experience that it left me with emotional scars that I would carry with me for decades. After my husband and I were married for a number of years, and we began to have some serious problems, I sought counseling, and it helped to some degree. But I never found the real freedom and healing that I so desperately needed. Then one day, I made a quality decision to live my life for Christ. I gave Him my broken heart and my broken life, and I asked Him to heal me, and to make me the person He created me to be. I knew that God had done a work in me, because I suddenly developed an insatiable hunger for His presence and His Word. I got up early every morning to pray, and to read the Scriptures. I poured my heart out to the Lord, asking Him to make Himself real to me. I don't know when it happened – I can't tell you the date or the time – but I realized one day that the deep pain and sorrow in my inner being was gone. I have to be honest and tell you that all that time, I hadn't been seeking healing for my emotions – I had been seeking God. And the troubled past that I thought would haunt me forever was wiped away by His healing hand.

The apostle Peter wrote: "May grace (God's favor) and peace (which is perfect well-being, all necessary good, all spiritual prosperity, and freedom from fears and agitating passions and moral conflicts) be multiplied to you in [the full, personal, precise, and correct] knowledge of God and of Jesus our Lord." (2 Peter 1:2 AMP) This verse reveals the supernatural power we tap into when we actively seek the Lord with our whole hearts. This kind of power isn't available to those who aren't fully committed to Christ. We can only plug into this kind of power when we make up our minds to wholeheartedly seek and serve God in good times and in bad. The apostle Paul had the right idea when he said: "[For my determined purpose is] that I may know Him [that I may progressively become more deeply and intimately acquainted with Him, perceiving and recognizing and understanding the wonders of His Person more strongly and more clearly], and that I may in that same way come to know the power outflowing from His resurrection." (Philippians 3:10 AMP) When we are this serious about our relationship with God, we will witness His mountain-moving power working on our behalf, even if that mountain is emotional baggage from our past.

I began smoking cigarettes when I was a young teenager. By the time I met my husband, Joe, in college, I had already been smoking many years, and I was addicted. Joe had never been a smoker, and he didn't want me to be one either, so he would throw my packs of cigarettes out the car window whenever he got the chance. We got engaged, and then married, and though everyone thought I had quit smoking, I felt compelled to sneak a smoke from time to time. After I surrendered my life to Christ, I noticed one day that the relentless cravings for cigarettes had vanished. It amazed me that I had been delivered from a 20-year-old addiction so suddenly and completely. The Bible says: "Where the Spirit of the Lord is, there is liberty (emancipation from bondage, freedom)." (2 Corinthians 3:17 AMP) When we surrender our lives to Christ for real, we open the door to supernatural healing, deliverance, and freedom. Have you been earnestly seeking freedom from an enslaving addiction or a painful past without success? Perhaps the Lord wants you to stop your fruitless efforts, and to simply begin seeking Him in a deeper way. His presence and His healing are waiting for you.

Lord, today I give You my broken heart, my broken dreams, and my broken life. Make them into something beautiful for Your glory. Fill me with a growing passion for Your presence and Your Word. Teach me to love You, seek You, and serve You the way You desire and deserve. Thank You that as I come to know You in a deeper way, I will draw closer to the victories and blessings that belong to me in Christ!

Promise-Power Point: God's will for me is total freedom and wholeness, and He will enable and equip me to walk in them as I make it my highest priority to know Him personally and intimately.

God's Got Another Option

"Wait for the Lord; be strong and take heart and wait for the Lord." Psalm 27:14 NIV

When my niece was getting married, I knew that I had to buy an especially nice dress for the occasion. My sister and her husband were going all out, and this wedding was going to be an extraordinary affair. My husband and I combed the mall dress shops for days, and I tried on more outfits than I could count. We narrowed our choices down to two lovely dresses, and even though I had been praying for God's wisdom and help, we still couldn't decide which one to purchase, so we bought both of them.

The big day was approaching fast, and I still didn't know which dress to wear. Then two days before the wedding, Joe and I were out shopping for some accessories when we noticed that the stores had gotten some new inventory. We both agreed that we should look over the new selections, and almost immediately, I spotted a gorgeous sparkly blue dress on one of the racks. As soon as I tried it on, I knew it was the dress that I was meant to wear to the wedding. Joe knew it, too. The day of the wedding, I got more compliments on that dress than any dress I've ever owned.

The Lord used this dress incident to teach me that sometimes, when we have a decision to make, we will think we have only a certain number of options to choose from, and if we're not careful, we will settle for second best. But if we wait on God – even to the last minute, if necessary – He will present us with yet another option, one that will prove to be infinitely better than all the others. If you are in the valley of decision today, ask the Lord, "Am I in danger of settling for less than Your best?"

Lord, forgive me for the times that I missed out on Your best for me because of my impatience. Give me a trusting heart that truly believes that You always want what is best for me, and that Your timing is always perfect. When I am tempted to act hastily and foolishly, remind me of what it could cost me. Thank You that as I exercise faith and patience, I will receive all that You have promised me! (Hebrews 6:12)

Promise-Power Point: God often has options for me that I am not aware of at first, but that He will reveal to me when I wait on Him for His perfect will and timing.

Complaints, Doubts, and Highest Purposes

"We are pressed on every side by troubles, but not crushed and broken. We are perplexed because we don't know why things happen as they do, but we don't give up and quit." 2 Corinthians 4:8 TLB

If you have ever felt isolated and alone because of your devotion to the Lord, I can relate to how you feel. So could the prophet Jeremiah. If we look closely at a conversation he had with the Lord in Chapter 15 of the Book of Jeremiah, we can gain some valuable insights that can greatly benefit us in our walk with God.

In verse 17 (NLT), Jeremiah tells the Lord: "I never joined the people in their merry feasts. I sat alone because Your hand was on me. I was filled with indignation at their sins." Have you ever stayed home alone, rather than see a questionable movie with friends or family? Have you ever refused to attend a party or gathering that might involve ungodly behavior? If so, then you have an idea of the sacrifices that Jeremiah made, all because of His devotion to the Lord. But look how the prophet challenges God in the next verse. "Why then does my suffering continue? Why is my wound so incurable? Your help seems as uncertain as a seasonal brook, like a spring that has gone dry." (v. 18 NLT) Here, Jeremiah complains about the Lord's apparent lack of help when he's in need.

One thing we can learn here is that we don't have to pretend with God. If we are hurting in some way – if we are angry, fearful, or confused – we can tell the Lord exactly what our true feelings are. Only then can we receive the comfort and strength from Him that we so desperately need. Scripture says: "The Lord is near to all who call upon Him, to all who call upon Him sincerely and in truth." (Psalm 145:18 AMP) We are being insincere with God when we try to pretend that we are perfectly fine, while our insides are in utter turmoil. That kind of strategy will distance us from the Lord, and we will never have the deeply personal and intimate relationship with Him that He longs for us to have.

Notice how God responds to Jeremiah's complaints: "If you return to Me, I will restore you so you can continue to serve Me. If you speak good words rather than worthless ones, you will be My spokesman." (v. 19 NLT) The Lord doesn't get angry at His servant, but He does rebuke him for his lack of faith. Jeremiah's heart is in danger of becoming hard. That's what doubt does to us. And that's why Scripture warns: "Blessed (happy, fortunate, and to be envied) is the man who reverently and worshipfully fears [the Lord] at all times [regardless of circumstances], but he who hardens his heart will fall into calamity." (Proverbs 28:14 AMP)

When we start to doubt God's dealings with us, we open ourselves up to attacks from the Destroyer, who Jesus said "comes only to steal and kill and destroy." (John 10:10 NIV) When we are struggling in our faith, we need to confess it to the Lord, and to ask Him to strengthen us and give us wisdom for the battle. The Savior said, "Blessed are those who don't doubt Me." (Matthew 11:6 TLB) When we refuse to doubt our God in tense situations, His best blessings will begin to flow into our lives, and even the devil himself will not be able to stop them.

As the Lord goes on to speak to Jeremiah about acting as His spokesman, He says: "You must influence them; do not let them influence you!" (v. 19 NLT) Here, God attempts to get His servant's focus off of himself and his problems, and onto his divine calling and purpose. Once we receive God's precious gift of salvation, why doesn't the Lord just take us to heaven? He leaves us here so that we can partner with Him for the expansion of His kingdom on earth – to help others experience the same rebirth and renewal that we've had through the Holy Spirit. We can't make a difference for God when we live like everyone else. Jesus put it this way: "Let Me tell you why you are here. You're here to be salt-seasoning that brings out the God-flavors of this earth. If you lose your saltiness, how will people taste godliness? You've lost your usefulness and will end up in the garbage." (Matthew 5:13 MSG)

As believers in Christ, God has extraordinary plans and purposes for our lives. But if we lose our focus, if we compromise our walk with God, we will become useless to Him, and we will live mediocre, meaningless lives. Today, will you put aside your complaints and doubts, and lay hold of the Lord's highest purposes for you?

Lord, when I am hurt, angry, or confused, help me to share my true feelings with You. Give me a trusting heart, and enable me to stand strong in times of temptation and trial. Thank You that as I am faithful to You, You will use me to touch and change lives for all eternity!

Promise-Power Point: When I live my life as a God-pleaser, instead of a people-pleaser, He will send me divine appointments and open doors of opportunity that will change the lives of others for their good and His glory.

"Discreet" Decisions

"A fool vents all his feelings, but a wise man holds them back." Proverbs 29:11 NKJV

When I was facing some potentially serious health problems some time ago, I decided to keep them largely between myself and God. Normally, in a situation like this one, I would tell all of my closest family members and friends, but this time, I told no one but my husband, Joe. At first, I didn't feel right about my decision, and I told myself things like – "You need to share this with your loved ones. They have a right to know, and they will pray for you." But every time I was tempted to tell someone, I got a "check" in my spirit, sensing the Lord was telling me "no". This strategy turned out to be the right one for me, as it enabled me to stand in faith for the favorable outcome that I received in the end.

When I think about the way I handled this situation, I think of the word, "discreet". It's not a popular term these days, but perhaps it should be. A good definition of "discreet" says: "Marked by, exercising, or showing prudence and wise self-restraint in speech and behavior." Unfortunately, our society today has taught us to say exactly what we feel when we feel it. Some people call this "venting". But look at what the Bible says about this subject: "A fool vents all his feelings, but a wise man holds them back." (Proverbs

29:11 NKJV) Sometimes, telling people our business is the last thing God wants us to do, because it can affect our faith and the outcome of our situation. If I had told my loved ones the scary situation I was facing, they would have sympathized with me. That doesn't necessarily sound like a bad thing, but it might have caused me to keep the focus on myself, and to feel sorry for myself, instead of keeping my focus on God and His promises, and resisting self-pity.

When others have an intimate knowledge of the trials we are going through, they will have certain expectations for our behavior that may hold us in bondage to our emotions. We may tend to feel sad or unsettled while they are around. We may unconsciously try to meet their negative expectations, when instead, God may be telling us – "Don't think like everyone else does." (Isaiah 8:11 NLT) Or, "Do not fear what they fear." (1 Peter 3:14 NIV) I found it so much easier to smile, joke, and be happy around those who had no idea of my mental anguish. The more I smiled and laughed, the more at ease I felt, and the more peace and joy I had in my heart. According to Scripture, when we lose our joy, we lose our strength. (Nehemiah 8:10) Once our strength begins to diminish, it's nearly impossible for us to stand in faith for the victory, and we lose out on the blessings and rewards that God had in store for us.

When we are tempted to share our problems with others, we need to first examine our motives. Do we want them to feel sorry for us? Do we want to see them fret and worry on our behalf? Perhaps we are trying to subtly tell them: "See you're not the only one with problems – I have problems, too. Don't count on me for help." These are all ungodly attitudes that can prevent us from receiving God's best in our situation. If you are facing troubling circumstances today, don't automatically assume that you should confide in all of your loved ones. Seek God's will about who you should share your concerns with. Your faith and your future may depend on it.

Lord, when trouble comes, help me to turn to You first. Give me the wisdom and self-control I need to share my concerns only with the people who will help me to receive Your best in my situation. Guard me from self-focus and self-pity, and give me the comfort and reassurance that can only come from You. Thank You that as I make "discreet" decisions, You will honor me with victory, success, and blessings of all kinds!

Promise-Power Point: If I will seek God's wisdom and guidance before I share my concerns with others, He will help me and lead me to receive the very best outcome for my situation.

About the Author

Since 1998, **J. M. Farro** has served as the devotional writer and prayer counselor for Jesusfreakhideout.com – one of the first and largest Christian music web sites in the world. Her mission is to help others to discover the life-changing power of having a deeply personal relationship with Christ.

Through devotionals, podcasts, blogs, and books – including the best-selling *Life on Purpose* devotional book series – she encourages others to fulfill their God-given purpose and potential. She and her husband, Joe, have two sons, and live in Nazareth, Pennsylvania.

J. M. Farro
P.O. Box 434
Nazareth, PA 18064

jmf@jmfarro.com
farro@jesusfreakhideout.com

www.jmfarro.com
www.jesusfreakhideout.com
www.littlejesusfreaks.com

NOTES

NOTES

Printed in Dunstable, United Kingdom